A Carefree War

The Hidden History of Australian WWII Child Evacuees

A Carefree War

The Hidden History of Australian WWII Child Evacuees

BIG SKY PUBLISHING
www.bigskypublishing.com.au

Ann Howard

Big Sky Publishing Pty Ltd

PO Box 303, Newport, NSW 2106, Australia

Phone: 1300 364 611

Fax: (61 2) 9918 2396

Email: info@bigskypublishing.com.au

Web: www.bigskypublishing.com.au

Cover design and typesetting: Think Productions

Printed in China by Asia Pacific Offset Ltd

National Library of Australia Cataloguing-in-Publication entry (pbk.)

Author: Ann Howard

Title: A Carefree War

ISBN: 978-1-925275-19-3 (paperback)

Subjects: Australian History, Child Evacuees, WWII

Dewey Number: See National Library for CIP data

Front cover images:

'Rabbit Boys' - Andrew Kyle (right) and brothers.

Cassie and Jim Thornley in a hand tinted photograph.

Warren and Peter Daley, Cessnock.

John, Marie and their mother Eileen, Glen Innes.

Evacuees Geoff Northcott and Ian Newton with Alan Wilkinson and neighbours on a rubber drive to help the war effort.

HMAS *Kuttabul* sinking in Sydney Harbour.

Bruce H Crawford aged about 18 months.

Queenie Ashton evacuated two of her children to Armidale

RDB Whalley with his three sisters, Armidale.

Back Cover:

Young Kevin Murphy races past Lion Island

Contents

Acknowledgements

The wave of voluntary evacuation of children around Australia from 1939/1945 is hidden history, despite long-standing public interest in WWII. To unearth it, I needed the warmth and generosity of the many contributors Australia wide, who gave me photos, newspaper cuttings and reminiscences, and I am very grateful. They are listed in the book.

When I gave public talks, the audience enriched me with ideas. Everyone was so encouraging, I was further inspired. I'd like to give a special mention to Andrew Kyle for his original story which planted the seed of the book in my mind, and my partner, Robert Bickerstaff for patient listening, editing and great advice as always. My boys continue as my best fans. Sadly Lincoln, my middle son passed away in March 2015, at aged only 46 and I will so miss his enthusiasm and intelligence. My good doctor, Helen Greer kept me alive and kicking. Among the many well versed archivists and historians who supported my research are Lindsay Read - Children's Services, Kate Riseley - Archivist at Shore School, Judy Grieve and the historians at Armidale. Associate Professor Bev Kingston, my respected mentor from university days encouraged me. Geoff Pritchard gave invaluable technical advice. The Vincent Fairfax Family Foundation for Trove is a boon to armchair researchers, without charge. And I can't forget Roma, ageing dog companion - her approving gaze is on me as I write!

When I came to Australia, and was naturalised in the 1970s, I was immediately drawn to her history. My books about women, drovers, the AWAS, child migrants and other hidden histories sold well and I was able to do more research. Everyone has a story and I love to tell it.

Although aware of the tremendous sacrifice of the Australian men and women in WWII, I believed the Australian home front relatively safe. It was only after Andrew's chance remark, Christmas 2013 that my eyes were opened to voluntary child evacuation. Australia's story of WWII is not complete without their stories.

Foreword

British TV has the so-called Hitler Channel for stark scene-setting from WWII. Less organised but still poignant in many ageing Australian minds are images of the Japanese invasion that very nearly happened.

1942 rises as the Year of the Panic, with stub-winged warplanes over tropical islands and Sydney people hastily selling their harbourside homes. I recall my father, that winter, setting off with military rifle and overcoat to look for fifth columnists said to be signalling out to sea by night, and his frightened determination to defend our farm against trained enemy soldiers.

1942 is the sudden start of unaccompanied train trips by children being sent inland to rural relations. Frightened mothers, whose menfolk were fighting in the islands made far-reaching decisions as to where the family, sometimes barely out of babyhood, might find refuge.

Ann Howard, herself a child evacuee from European hostilities, records the shifts and displacements of a time when governments did little for the civilian population except lie to it through censored media. She details the largest upheaval since white settlement from oral memoirs and box camera photos, all placed within frameworks of history

Les Murray

Introduction

Fear of losing your country, the red dirt beneath your feet, is a very real, breathless fear. Australian women, whose men had gone overseas to fight in WWII, paused at the sink and watched their children laughing at play in the back yard. It was unthinkable that Australia could be invaded. Yet after Pearl Harbour, then the fall of Singapore to the Japanese on 15 February, 1942, it was a sickening possibility. As they brushed their children's hair in the evening, they wondered what was going to become of them. The Rape of Nanking in the old Chinese capital, by the Japanese in 1938 had left them in no doubt what would happen to civilians in the path of that Army.

The Japanese Imperial Army moved swiftly up the Malay Peninsula, 'take all, kill all', with a crab claw threat towards the island of Australia. The conflict that had echoed in distant Britain was now on their doorstep. Scanning smudgy, censured newsprint to try and find out what was happening, women on the home front in Australia whispered to their mothers and sisters that they thought the Japanese Imperial Army was going to invade. But where? Geraldton, Western Australia? Port Kembla? Sydney Harbour? Newcastle? Armidale? Hobart? Or up at the top of Australia? Yes! That's where it would happen.

Troops had been sent up to the Atherton Tablelands and the Queensland Government had evacuated civilians. They would probably relinquish the top of Australia to the Japanese, was their reasoning. It was mythical, but it was called the Brisbane Line. It was happening - sisters and girlfriends had donned Service uniforms and some were secretive about their postings. Japanese lightning raids were not reported in the Press, so civilians became cynical about official information. Wherever they thought the Japanese might land on the coast, or pick a target, they wanted to get their children away safely away to the mountains and inland.

Like animals that drag their young to a safe place away from predators, they did not wait for official sanction; they fled, in their thousands. The beach became a dangerous barbed-wired place, the Sydney Harbour a netted area. Irrational decisions were made; children were evacuated to Lithgow, where the Small Arms Factory was, and Lithgow children in turn where evacuated away.

As children were hastily dressed and bundled into trucks and cars, they had no idea of the grim reality of the situation. They thought they were going on holiday. They would have a carefree war.

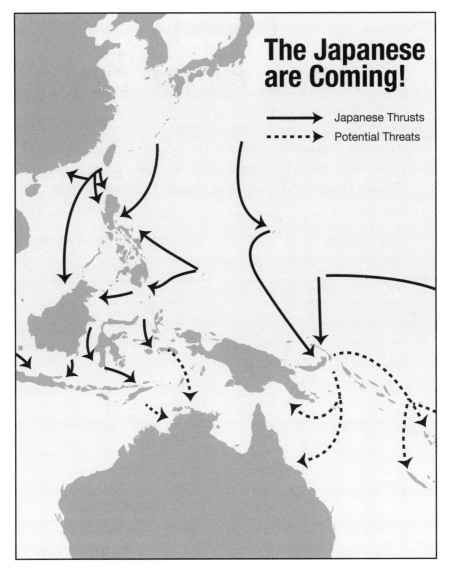

The Japanese are Coming!

→ Japanese Thrusts

┄┄► Potential Threats

Chapter 1
I was a Rabbit Boy.

Little Andrew, wandering the Oberon farm, found a rusty motorbike on its side in a back paddock. He stood staring at it for a while, thinking ... **If only I could find a couple of wheels, I'd be out of here!**

Chapter 1

In Australia, families clustered round the wireless heard Robert Menzies' announcement on the evening of 3 September, 1939: 'Fellow Australians! It is my melancholy duty to inform you that in consequence of the persistence of Germany in the invasion of Poland, Great Britain has declared war on her and that as a result, Australia is also at war'.

Meryl Hanford remembers her relative's plans:
> The government seemed unconcerned in the 40s and it was left to people to make private arrangements about their children.

Andrew Kyle remembers his evacuation experience as a 'rabbit boy':
> Due to the Japanese scare, I was sent to Oberon from 1940-41 with my brothers. When we came back home, people didn't question where myself and my elder brother had been for nine months. My parents knew these people and we'd been invited to stay in their old shack on about 100 acres. We went up there in an old 'Whippet', loaded up to the roof. When the old man saw the state of the place, he cooked up a story about an urgent recall to the city (for him).

> The iron roof was lined with chaff bags with creatures running along inside. There were no doors, just bits of hessian hanging down. It was six miles out of town along Shooters Hill Road. If you wanted to move anything, there were some old wooden sleds and moth-eaten nags you had to catch and harness up to do so. Peas were the cash crop. A couple of hard-bitten daughters sat in rocking chairs on the veranda taking pot shots at the birds. There was a wind up gramophone, with one record for entertainment. My younger brother was about two years old and still in nappies - we had to change him when we couldn't stand it anymore - my older brother usually did that!

> The lady of the house was a short order cook in the town and she left in the sulky before dawn. For breakfast we'd have a bit of bread to toast smeared with butter or dripping. We had no electricity so we would need to get the fire going first and our toaster was a fork made from a bit of fencing wire. There was a Coolgardie safe and a chip heater. Water was always scarce. Ma, the old lady, put our

little brother in the corner of her room on a palliasse. He woke up to hear a tinkling noise and it was Ma on the 'po'.

'What are you staring at?!' she would yell.

He hid under his blanket. We were rabbit boys.

The old bloke was a bush carpenter and went away putting up sheds for people. He only had one eye, but he knew where the traps made from loops of fencing wire were. He had a very sharp knife. There were lots of snakes as we walked the property and we were warned to keep away. We boys were from the city and stood aghast as he grabbed a screaming rabbit and cut its head off. He'd ring the paws and deglove the rabbit of its skin. These were sold to make Akubra hats. They had a few mangy dogs, which were thrown the carcases. Every night we had rabbit for dinner, every way you could think of - roast, stewed, fried.

The strainers on the water tanks had long rusted away. They tipped the tanks on their sides and we were small enough to crawl through the holes and scoop out the sediment. There were remains of reptiles, birds and small mammals in the mud. The family said the water never tasted the same after the tank was cleaned out! It was a bit difficult to have a bath as water was always at a premium. As it got near Christmas, the old man went out and grabbed one of the mangy looking chooks and cut its head off. It was running around with blood spurting for what seemed like forever. Another thing I've never fancied eating! One time, they fattened a pig up, killed it and put it in a bath of salt. They didn't really know what they were doing. You couldn't eat the meat so they buried it in the end.

They had a dog that was tied up on about six foot of chain because it had savaged a sheep years ago. It was tied up for punishment then just left in the sun and snow. You couldn't go near it, poor thing. A cow wandered into the quicksand and my brother had to run the six miles into Oberon for help. By the time people came with ropes, the poor cow had disappeared. There was an old motorbike, rusty, with both wheels missing in one of the paddocks. I used to stare at it and think, 'If I could find two wheels, I'd be out of here'. Two Italians, classed as enemy aliens, Vincento and Arnaldo, were sent to the farm for two days here and there. We looked forward to them coming as they were really nice guys. Sometimes a pile of comics would arrive that had been sent by relatives and that was bliss.

Andrew had fun on the Oberon farm, as children usually do. Many child evacuees had a blissful time in the country, being spoilt by grandmas, aunts, uncles, cousins and friends, able to disappear into the paddocks, dropping into bed exhausted to sleep soundly.

The *Australian Women's Weekly*, December 27, 1941 reported, 'In every coastal city in Australia this last fortnight, one question has run like a refrain through the news and rumours of war. It is: What are we going to do about the children? Ever since Europe felt the full horror of aerial warfare, the plight of children has aroused the indignation of men and women. Now, when Australia is in imminent danger, hundreds and thousands of parents are thinking mainly of one problem - the safety of their youngsters'.

Councils had interminable meetings and mostly decided that there was no future in voluntary evacuation, that it must be funded and compulsory. But how would they enforce it?

Col (Colin) Gammidge was a child evacuee who left Merrylands to go up-line to his small country town birthplace.

Dad was an NES warden in Excelsior Street, Merrylands, and we had an air raid trench in the backyard. The school (Granville Primary) had concrete shelters in the playground and windows taped with brown sticky tape. I got to see the Japanese submarine after it was recovered from the Harbour and we also went alongside the Queen Mary which was a troopship at the time. I can also remember going through the submarine net to get to Manly in the ferry and how scary it felt to be on the wrong side of the net! We had lots of blackouts and the NES wardens would check that lights didn't show in the street. There were few cars.

In 1942 my mother took my elder brother Ray and I back to the tiny town, Barmedman, where I was born in 1936. In Barmedman I went to the one-teacher school. I think we stayed in Barmedman for three months or so. Mum's family came from the area and Dad was an 'import' being a railway bloke from Newcastle. I remember when Mum came back to take Ray and me home to Sydney, all I wanted was a 'milkman's book' which is apparently a small black notebook for keeping accounts.

Barmedman lies north of Temora between Wyalong and Temora. Our relation, Merv Hill, had a farm outside Barmedman called 'Sunnyside' and a house in town.

The farm 'Sunnyside' is just south of the town heading towards Reefton. There were amazing place names like 'Stockinbingal' and 'Gidginbung' - Dad knew them all in exact sequence being a 'railie' bloke of long standing. One day we hit a sheep along the line south of Sunnyside and my grandfather, Albert York, went back the next day, gave it a kick in the ribs whereupon it stood up and trotted off. We wondered if it would have lain there until death or figured out that it was still alive. Albert York ran the railway pumping station at Wyalong (Central), pumping water from a dam into those large overhead water tanks that dotted the country rail system to replenish the tenders of steam engines

At school we were told about sabre toothed tigers and I remember being terrified there was one in the dark end of the house veranda in De Boos Street, Barmedman. Wheat was the main export from the town and I remember horse-drawn wagons and trucks loaded with bagged wheat at the silo. The trip to Barmedman was a real trek in those days. The Southern Mail (I think?) took you to Cootamundra then you changed to the two car rail motor which was not air-conditioned, a hot trip after the mail train.

Eileen Pye left Sydney for Naradhan, late January, 1942:
Naradhan was the end of the line going west. My husband's young sister was sent from Sydney to stay with her relatives near Mudgee at

the same time. The train left Central (Sydney) at 8 pm and we arrived at Naradhan at 4 o'clock Friday afternoon. By that time we were the only passengers in the only carriage, two thirteen year old girls and an eleven year old boy. The train had disconnected carriages along the way. The reverse happened on the way back to Sydney. I left in September 1943, a 14 year old girl. My cousins stayed until end of school year. I was the only passenger when the train left Naradhan, travelling overnight and arriving at Central about 8 pm. I think my 'Uncle' would have tipped the guard to keep an eye on me. By the time the train arrived in Sydney it had reattached carriages at different stations and it was overcrowded with soldiers sitting in the corridors.

In the UK, many city evacuees had never seen a cow or breathed fresh air, and were frightened when they saw the sea. Australian children who were evacuated could run free, play with animals and bring home butter, fresh eggs, and fruit in season, jams and flowers. For some this would be one of the most memorable times of their lives - for all the right reasons!

Cecily Atton:

My sister and I were sent by our parents from Sydney to our aunts and uncles in Narrabri in 1942. We were around fourteen. The food was wonderful - everything was fresh. When school was over, we were out and around on the farm — but had to be careful of snakes. The hens were free range and made nests all over and you had to be careful in case the snake had got there first when you collected eggs!

Anthony Healy remembers a time in 1942, his dad was in the army and his mother was a cleaner:

We lived in Wilson St. Redfern opposite the Eveleigh Workshops an enemy target if ever there was one. We had a boarder who had spent a considerable time in the bush. I am not quite sure of the relationship between him and my parents but they seemed close. At some stage he must have suggested to my mother that it might be a good idea to take my brother and me to the bush. I cannot recall the events of our departure but I'm sure it had to be by train to Orange. How we got from Orange to our Bark Hut on the Ophir Road, I cannot recall. Yes, it was a bark hut with a dirt floor. I cannot recall any building of the hut so I assume it was already there when we arrived. Possibly something our boarder James Lawrence (Grandad) knew about.

The beds were made of four 'Y' posts, with the sides being two poles with a hessian bag threaded on them to provide a mattress. We were located slightly off the road, but on the other side was a house and land owned by a Mr and Mrs Freeman. A river ran through the back of their property. They had a rather belligerent goat that had me completely bluffed, some sheep and I remember lambs being de-tailed and castrated. And there were beehive boxes on the land. Mrs Freeman had a baby while we were there. I was seven at the time and my brother John had his sixth birthday there. Mum came up for a visit and it may have been for John's birthday.

We set traps for possums and I was on a kangaroo hunt with Mr Freeman and his two dogs. We had kangaroo tail soup that night. I did go back some years ago to view the place but the hut was gone and mum said it had burnt down. Things were much smaller than I remember. Down the road from us was a waterfall that may have only been a set of rapids. Nearby was another hut whose occupant was a Mr Ferguson, known as 'Old Fergie'. At one stage Mr Freeman was making coke using a large iron container which sat on the side of the road.

Mr Freeman organised with a man to move his beehives into Orange. The night before the move, the mouth of the hives were stuffed with bags so the bees couldn't get out the next morning. Jim Lawrence was helping Mr Freeman move the hives on to his truck or dray. I was watching from a distance when all of a sudden Jim Lawrence dropped the hive he was carrying and ran off. In carrying the hive he had worked the bag out of the mouth and the bees came storming out. He referred to the bees as those 'black Italian buggers'.

Chapter 1

I do remember coming back from a trip in a buggy and the arms of the buggy came out of the harness and it tipped up and sat us in a puddle of water. We lost a year of schooling and when we came back were a year behind what we would have been had we stayed. During the time away was when the Japanese submarines were in the Harbour. Mum slept through the siren and woke up at the 'All Clear!'

John Squires recalls his experience in Muswellbrook:

In January 1942, as a ten and half year-old boy I was dispatched from Paddington, with my six year-old brother, by mother to remote Muswellbrook, less than 80 miles from the coast. My great-uncle worked for the PMG and we lived with him where he boarded in Scott Street. We spent three months there, went to school, played in the Hunter River (which was not flowing), climbed peppermint trees and generally had a good time. As the Japs didn't invade, we came back home after three months in time to survive the shelling, such as it was, of the Eastern Suburbs later in 1942.

I recall when I was eight years old the special night edition on the declaration of war against Germany in September 1939, which mainly dealt with the sizes of the competing armies and navies. My point here is there was fear and concern by 1942 as we didn't know what would happen to us here in 'far away' Australia, since we had been fairly mercilessly bombed in Darwin and Broome in February of that year. And, though properly censored, the newspapers and radio still gave us sufficient news to unsettle. I never asked my mother, a single parent, why she had sent us away. It was on reflection a most unusual action as she sent her sons but kept her 15 year-old-daughter home. This was possibly because she had left school and was earning some wages and perhaps just because she was a girl.

My brother and I went to Muswelbrook in late January 1942, before the Darwin bombings, so there must have been powerful reasons for this action. Of course Pearl Harbour and the sinking of the *Prince of Wales* and *Repulse* in December 1941 were reported in all their horror by early 1942. Was my mother's action an opportunity to use her uncle's presence at work in Muswellbrook, or merely an opportunity to show her concern to protect her boys?

In respect to my time in Muswellbrook, I recall the first day our landlady asked us if we liked egg sandwiches. As we did, we got them for the whole three months and after returning to Sydney, I foreswore them for many years.

As I learned later my future wife, (then a nine year old), was equipped to travel to Gunning with overalls, a packed bag, and a rubber around her neck for shellshock, but her mother couldn't bear to part with her (until her daughter and I married in the fifties).

Charmaine Williams:

My parents and I had lived at Maroubra since 1939. From 1941 and into 1942 the Japanese were patrolling the east coast, and we were often woken at night by loud explosions, the sky criss-crossed by searchlights. The Japanese were trying to destroy Bunnerong Power Station and General Motors Holden, which was producing aeroplane parts, guns and twenty-five pounders. Older children were out early mornings trying to find the long strips of silver foil, dropped from RAAF planes overnight. It interfered with radar being sent from the Japanese ships - the radar signals bounced back instead of honing in on a particular target. The beaches were strung with wicked looking barbed-wire and all the steps along the beachfront had been destroyed to stop the Japanese having easy access to the city. Street signs were removed. Yet life went on.

'Dad's Army' was out in force every evening to patrol the streets, making sure not a chink of light escaped from behind the blackout screens. They carried red buckets of sand to put out any spot fires. As the shelling increased, it was decided I should be sent away to family friends who lived at Werombi, about 26 kilometres from Camden. I was an only child, nearly five, and it was not till I was older I realised my parents must have been heartbroken at having to send me away not knowing what the future would hold. As a city child, I was absolutely in seventh heaven on the farm, a wonderful freedom which was not possible in Maroubra. Orderly rows of orange trees with their sweet smelling blossoms were fun to run between. I collected warm brown eggs which the hens laid in odd places, (they were free range), and it was wonderful to see warm milk spurting into the pail from the two cows, Strawberry and Violet. All lovely warm animal smells.

'Auntie Doll' and 'Uncle Oliver' had cleared their 40 acre block by hand, lived in a tent 'till their home was built, then planted groves of oranges, mandarins, quinces and plums. Auntie Doll was an excellent cook and preserver. The cranky old fuel stove produced all sorts of goodies. It must have been very hot for her in the summer heat. The churned butter tasted quite different from the small pats of butter we received on our ration cards. The pantry shelves were lined with clear Fowler jars of fruits and vegetables for out of season eating. Uncle Oliver was a small hard working man, and I followed him everywhere, bringing his morning tea down into the bottom paddock where we shared warm sultana cakes. I even walked with the stump jump plough which the beautiful Clydesdale horse, Bonnie, pulled through the rich brown earth. Monkey Creek ran through the property, and it was fun to have a swim in the crystal clear water on a hot day.

After some months when things settled down, I returned home to my loving parents. However I will never forget that amazing time at Werombi, and afterwards I spent many happy school holidays at the farm.

Don McKern:

We were at the farm over winter 1942 and it was very cold at times. One of my morning jobs was to climb the tank stand, and break the ice on top, so the water would run. One morning as I climbed back down the ladder, there on the blanket where my dear little sister was sunning herself on, was a small brown snake curled up beside her. Without any thought I flattened its head with the hammer I had just used to break the ice! Later I was told it was a death adder.

Anthony Euwer:

We lived two doors from the Mayfield Monastery. They had a large, undeveloped paddock which was little boy's heaven, with bushes, trees, pathways and a quarry. The night the Japanese mini-submarine shelled Newcastle, the only damage I was aware of was to one of my climbing trees over the quarry in the Monastery less than a hundred feet away! A shell had hit the base of the tree and demolished it without exploding. I have since discovered that most of the shells failed to explode. I gather the raid was meant to demoralise more than damage, but it failed on all counts. We stayed in Mayfield for a few weeks, but eventually went back to Denman, just in case. We needn't have bothered.

Following is an example of an advertisement for evacuees from the 1940s. Not all were as stylish as this one from Armidale:

SUITABLE FOR EVACUEES TO COUNTRY

Excellent New England Freehold Property, 124 acres, together with fine large Gentleman's Residence, of hardwood weatherboard, on outer rim of town of Armidale, comprising 8 rooms and long verandahs. Tennis court. Electric light, telephone, water laid on. Stables, sheds, man's room, garages, and large orchard. All wire-netted and subdivided. On main road. University and good schools in this fine country town. Price £2,500.

To evacuees going inland, life was a holiday and the majority of those with a story remember the time away with pleasure. More than one evacuee has said to me, 'It was the best time of my life!'

Chapter 2
Cherry Blossom Land

There was a picture in the Sydney Morning Herald *from the 30s, we found under the lino when we were changing the floor covering, of a Japanese cruiser, the* Shintoka Maru, *sailing up the Harbour. All the sailors lined the deck with cameras. My parents said they were 'checking the lay of the land'.*

– Meryl (Johnstone) Hanford

A Carefree War

It would be fair to say that suspicions of Japanese intentions were exacerbated due to most Australians never having seen a Japanese person, and few Australians having visited Japan. Australians had a picture postcard image of Japan, however Japanese tourists were reported to police as spies by nervous civilians, as they photographed everything and bought maps which was seen as early evidence of Japan's growing desire to colonise.

In 1935, there were 88,176 Japanese pearl divers, gardeners, traders, merchant navy officers, and government officials living in the Asia-Pacific region, but few lived in Australia and intermarriage was rare. In May 1942, the Melbourne *Argus* said, 'If the Japanese had wings instead of arms, or fishtails instead of legs, it might be easier to understand them. In observing people who read newspapers, smoke cigarettes, and go to the 'pictures', we naturally think they are like us. And we are quite baffled when we realise they are quite different underneath. It is failure to consider these differences which has made so many of our 'experts' views about the present war with Japan hopelessly inaccurate. Inside Japan itself there is depressing evidence that the people, few of whom know why the war is being fought, simply accept it as they have always accepted earth-quakes, typhoons, poverty, and other evils of life.' The Australian perception of Japan in the Press changed drastically over the war period. The following newspaper articles spanning 21 years begin and end with the theme of cherry blossom, as they tell a story.

The *Daily Telegraph*, Launceston, 5 December, 1925 asked coyly 'Would you live in a land of paper kites, cherry blossoms, and festivals? Of such is the land of Japan. In Japan, charm of manner is the keynote to character, and everyone you meet is most beautifully polite. Grace and dignity of bearing are cultivated from babyhood ... There are gay festivals, lanterns lit, and the boys' festival, when every boy, from babies to old men, fly their paper kites. Living in Japan is like living in a coloured picture book that never has an end!'

By 1935, the tone begins to change and criticisms of the Japanese way of life begin to creep into news reports. The *Albury Banner* of 15 February, reports Japan as 'Topsy Turvey Land', '...67 million of them, "virile, happy, family loving, athletic, profound, Emperor Worshippers", and yet...'

Chapter 2

By 1942, James R Young, an American journalist imprisoned by the Japanese for 'spreading false news and rumours', wrote a blistering article for the *Sunday Times*, Perth, 5 April, about what army fanatics had done to the people of Japan. 'The war with China had cut one eighth of an inch from matches, as wood was a war material, there were scarcities of food ... no bright floral kimonos or make-up for women, hardly any private vehicles on the road and 260 forbidden imports. Steel gramophone needles were banned, dance halls closed and the radio played military music constantly. The radio announcers attacked Chinese, British and Americans as being warlike and aggressive, forcing Japan to defend itself by invading China. Resident foreigners resigned themselves to be constantly spied on and cherry blossom tourism had almost entirely disappeared.'

Towards the end of the war, pilots of the Cherry Blossom Squadrons were trained to guide *ohka* rocket-powered glider bombs into American ships (*ohka* means 'cherry blossom' in Japanese), and each *ohka* weapon, containing 2,800 pounds of explosives, had cherry blossom painted on its nose.

Post war, Peter V Russo in *The Argus,* Melbourne, 23 February, 1946 was pleading for fraternisation, although he knew people had suffered the brutality of Japanese captors: 'It is well to remember that Australia's aloofness from the outside world, particularly in the Asiatic sphere, was responsible for our alarming state of unpreparedness a few years ago.'

By 1946, marriages between servicemen and Japanese women were being celebrated and the tourists were admiring the cherry blossom.

The accepted view of Japan's emergence as a modern power is from the second arrival of Commodore Perry and the twelve black ships, ending the isolation of Japan when, observing guns firing at the emperor's palace, the Japanese realised their regression from 200 years of isolation. Despite isolation, their idea of an Empire started before the scramble to industrialisation. In the 1880s, the Japanese government allowed labourers to work in their colonies and some western countries, to become useful contacts. Due to the White Australia Policy only a limited number arrived in Australia. Thousands of impoverished rural girls saw their chance to escape poverty, but only as prostitutes. Mostly dead before the age of thirty, they were tricked, kept indebted and given drugs; the usual sad story. The Japanese government objected to these women seeking work, as it reflected badly on Japan, and introduced fines and imprisonment for the girls and people trading in them.

An interesting view concerning these women is the government statement, 'If Imperial Japan aims to be a supreme power in the East, a wealthy and militarily strong country, and furthermore, to spread its righteousness to the four corners of the world, the presence of many young Japanese girls living in conditions worse than slavery, will stain the Japanese flag for a long time', as quoted by Bill Mihalopoulos in his book *Sex in Japan's Globalization 1870 to 1930*.

The real impetus to expand as distinct from the desire, came with Japan's modern economy emerging in 1853, after *kaikin*, a policy of limited trade and diplomatic relations, had given a long period of peace. Japan had developed busy cities, thriving agriculture, domestic trade, wage labour instead of peasantry, increasing literacy and a print culture, laying a strong base for a modern economy. Numbers of Germans moved into influential positions to achieve this. To fuel this economy, Japan, with few natural resources, needed coal, oil, iron, copper, lead, tin, zinc, rubber and rice.

Other nations, like Britain, had built empires to secure natural resources for prosperity and the Japanese copied them. When they became the first Asian nation to defeat a European country, in the Russo-Japanese war of 1904-05 (utilising German military advice and new technology), the slogan 'Asia for the Asians' was coined. Their government became increasingly dominated by the powerful army and navy (there was no separate air force). Modernisation did not challenge subjugation to their emperor, as someone to obey as a god destined to rule the world, but reinforced it.

The stage was set for expansionism. Factions within the armed forces struggled for power. The Imperial Japanese Navy made its own decision to invade Germany's territories of the Marianas, Carolinas, Palau and Marshall Islands in 1914. Japan justified expanding its fleet and doubling the army budget, after securing South Pacific and

Chapter 2

Indian Ocean sea lanes from 1914 to 1918. She now emerged as an international power.

However, despite the success of its light industry, Japan had a debtor-nation status, resented by the population. Japan was also aggrieved at the little she received from the peace settlements. In an attempt at slowing military build up in the interests of peace, the *Washington Naval Agreement of 1922* only allowed Japan one ship to Britain's five, causing resentment. Japan later withdrew from the *London Naval Treaty*, another peace attempt. Planning started on the giant battleships of the Yamato class.

Tensions in society between the Japanese government, forces and civilians were eased during the twenties when, as in the fragile Weimar Republic in Germany, urban architecture, literature, fashion, popular music and film blossomed. As East met West in Tokyo and Yokohama, women with bobbed hair congregated in cafes enjoying western jazz. Jascha Heifetz, the violinist, played to huge audiences. The Japanese, greedy for outside culture, proudly developed versions of their own. Glittering patrons attended 'Nippon Modern films', now competing with highly capitalised foreign film companies. Then the Great Kanto Earthquake of 1923 and the following tsunami swept away this vibrant community, when about 140,000 died, buildings were ruined and artworks lost. With reconstruction, militarism flourished on discontent. Dissidents were silenced as happened in Germany, some for good. Women wore kimonos decorated with tanks and children played war games. War was in the air.

The belief in the 'Empire of the Sun' was reinforced. In 1927, the Tanaka Memorial, stated in part, '... in order to conquer the world, we must first conquer China...' These words are generally regarded as fraudulent, however, when the silk trade collapsed, with thousands of peasants losing work, Japan's foreign policy did focus on China. The Japanese became entrenched in right-wing politics with government promises of improved living standards. The domination of the rest of Asia became a matter of Japanese public interest and was seen as their divine right.

As Japan asserted itself over China, Great Britain, France and the United States, with the power to check aggression, failed to, merely closing borders with Hong Kong and Burma. In September 1931, Japanese forces challenged the League of Nations authority, invading Inner Manchuria in northern China. The Japanese puppet government of Manchukuo was not recognised. In February 1932, Japan withdrew from the League of Nations.

Widely reported in the Australian Press in detail, and noted by anxious civilians, was the behaviour of the Japanese Imperial Army in China. After Japan's subjugation of Shanghai, Nanking, (the then Chinese capital), was captured in November 1937, the 'Rape of Nanking' following. Australians read how for over six weeks, undisciplined Japanese soldiers were left to loot and pillage, declaring 'kill all, take all' in the surrounded city, some boasting of numbers of citizens killed each day. Exact figures are debatable, but thousands were killed, women raped, mutilated and countless children and babies murdered. Barbarous incidents by Japanese soldiers, only a few of whom were tried later, were photographed and reported to the world Press by missionaries and Europeans, caught in the mayhem. The 'Rape of Nanking' marked a vicious change in Japanese military strategy that would become infamous in the Pacific War and definitely accelerate evacuation on the home front.

Cynthia Fisher (nee Reinhold):

We, as a family, lived at Wavell Heights, a suburb of Brisbane. My mother voluntarily evacuated myself and my older brother from Brisbane during the war. The story going around was, apparently, that the Japanese were coming and would be raping the women and bayoneting the babies. As I was a baby at the time, born September 1940, it was decided to take us to Inglewood, where we were billeted with a family, a Mrs Calligan or O'Calligan, very close to the Condamine River. I have no memory whatsoever of this, I was too young. But my brother, born May 1934, now unfortunately deceased, had lots of memories.

There were a few children in the family, and these country children took delight in making life difficult for the city boy. They were playing ball and threw it into a bindi patch, and told my brother it was his turn to go and get it. They thought it was a great joke.

My mother told me she was very worried about me crawling around through the dirt and dust that was everywhere. Mum and Keith were very pleased when it was again declared safe to return to Brisbane.

Japanese ambitions led to conflict with the United States of America, who became her arch enemy. In spite of its formal recognition of the Vichy government, the United States, Japan's best trading partner, imposed a total embargo on steel, oil and gasoline in August 1941. The Japanese military discussed invading India to plunder her riches but Australia was thought preferable, not only aligned with the arch enemy, but available to them as a Pacific base.

As the American navy was an obstacle to Japan's expansionism, on Sunday, 7 December, 1941, Japanese planes bombed the US fleet in Pearl Harbour, destroying half of it. The Americans immediately joined the Allies in World War II.

As a previous ally, Japan had an uneasy relationship with Australia. In the *War Precautions Regulation* of 1916, all Japanese were required to register as aliens. Japan and Australia had collected intelligence from the mid-nineteenth century, *The Times* correspondents using the telegraphic link between Tokyo and London which was slow, expensive and censored by the Japanese, had shared it with Australia.

In the 1920s and 30s a remarkable collection of international Japan enthusiasts and journalists worked for the *North China Standard* and the *Japan Times*. A George Gorman, became a pro-Japanese propagandist and was imprisoned in Tokyo, accused of espionage, but later employed by the British government. Another, Charles Dunn, an academic, was awarded the Order of the Rising Sun for promoting the Japanese language. Journalists lived in dangerous times, some tortured and murdered by the police.

In Australia, information was collected en masse by Japanese students, traders and merchant navy officers. Civilians were well aware of this and uneasy about it. The Director of Government Railways in Japan requested a map of the city of Sydney from the Town Hall in June 1919 and not only did the Town Clerk respond obsequiously to the flattery, he volunteered a map of the drainage systems as well!

A Carefree War

From the City Surveyor's Office, (signed by the city surveyor):

I forward herewith a Map of the City of Sydney which could be forwarded to the Director of Government Railways in Japan in response to his request. For fuller information regarding this City, a copy of the Vade Mecum (manual), could be sent. As to the system of development, it seems to me that requests might be made to the Premier for a copy of the Greater Sydney Bill and to the Water and Sewerage Board for information as to the development of water and drainage systems...

The Town Clerk to the Secretary of the Water Board:

Dear Sir, I have the honour to inform you that the Lord Mayor of Sydney has received a request from the Director of the Imperial Government Railways of Japan, Tokyo, asking for information ... and I should be glad if you could forward me a copy of the Souvenir which was issued by your Board, some time ago ...

Requests to help improve their infrastructure by examining the best systems in developed countries were flattering in tone and it worked. Piecemeal information was useful. Darwin continued to be a centre of interest and navy personnel asked if aboriginal people could perform manual labour. In an article in the *Journal of the Australian War Memorial* in 1987, Bob Walton established firmly that the Japanese Navy had spied on the coast.

Archives reveal a constant flow of requests from Japanese local and central government authorities, consulates and firms. One query in 1910 concerned training of naval cadets, another in December 1919 by the Japanese Consul in Sydney, was for a panoramic view of Melbourne for their education department. Requests in the 1920s and 1930s were about agricultural policy, communism, maps and government statistics, and continued into the war period with the Commonwealth Parliamentary Library being asked for land maps and air charts for Australia and British Islands in the Pacific! The Japanese Consul-General 1934-1935, was given a detailed report (provided by the Department of the Interior), on Canberra's water system.

Like ostriches, many authoritative figures refused to acknowledge what was plainly obvious. Visiting United States geography professor

Ellsworth Huntington wrote in 1923 that he was surprised 'how many intelligent Australians were concerned over this matter'.

As WWII approached, sampans to the north of Australia were scrutinised. If Japanese Mandated Islands were taken as a base, it was calculated 50 sampans could enter Australian waters with 3,750 Japanese. Dossiers were open on every Japanese person in the Commonwealth. Interpreters who could be trusted were sought.

On February 14, 1942, the Japanese Navy initiated plans at their Imperial Headquarters to invade Australia. Captain Tomioka of the Naval Staff's pressing for the taking of Australia with a token force was labelled 'so much gibberish' in the Imperial General Headquarters' secret diary. Prime Minister Tojo rejected the plan because huge distances in Australia meant stretched supply lines, open to enemy attack. There was a divergence of opinion between the navy and army and within both bodies. The navy contended that Japan should push forward. They were aware of the increasing flow of American war materials, especially aircraft, to Australia, indicating allied intent to use it as a counter-offensive base. The navy insisted that Japan be actively on the offensive, attacking Australia for her wool, wheat, chemicals, meat, and fertilizers.

The world's three largest navies in 1939 belonged to the United States, Great Britain and Japan. The Japanese navy was overconfident from its recent successes. The Japanese army, however, strongly opposed over commitment, rejecting the proposed invasion as a reckless undertaking far in excess of Japan's capabilities, contending the required 12 combat divisions would weaken other fronts and available shipping was unequal to transport.

From *Senshi Sosho* the official Japanese war history published by the Japanese Defence Agency, we learn that: 'The Navy High Command wanted to invade Australia, in order to eliminate it as a potential springboard for a counter-offensive by the Allies, but the army baulked at this as requiring an excessive commitment of manpower'.

Australia's Army Commander-in Chief, General Thomas Blamey, 'remained confident' of holding Australia. He later wrote: 'Had the Japanese wished to seize it, Western Australia, with its vast potential wealth, might have fallen an easy prey to them in 1942. While it would have extended their commitment to a tremendous degree, it would have given them great advantages.'

The capture of the Australian administered islands New Britain and New Ireland during the first operational stage of Japan's Pacific aggression was to be followed by the capture of Port Moresby in the Australian Territories of Papua and Tulagi in the British Solomon Islands. There was clear intention of the Japanese invading sovereign Australian territory before Pearl Harbour. At an Imperial Liaison Conference held in Tokyo on 10 January, 1942, the Japanese army supported a plan to isolate Australia from the United States, known as Operation FS, the aim of which was to 'throttle Australia into submission' with a tight blockade, using psychological pressure, presumably, behind the sporadic shelling and bombing of different locations.

Immediately following the fall of Singapore on February 15, 1942, Army Chief of Staff General Sugiyama advised his Japanese navy opposite number Admiral Nagano: '... it is useless for us to plan for an invasion of only part of Australia.'

As the British had their backs against the wall, John Curtin's appeal to the nation was in all the newspapers. The *Melbourne Herald,* 26 December, 1941: '...Without any inhibitions of any kind I make it quite clear that Australia looks to America, free of any pangs as to our traditional links or kinship with the United Kingdom'. This sent shock waves across the world as a disloyal rejection of Britain; but it was a bold statement of Australia's increasingly desperate position. Japanese bombers attacking Darwin in February 1942 raised fears even more. The Curtin cabinet had appealed for help to British Prime Minister Winston Churchill and to US president Franklin Roosevelt even before the fall of Malaya, New Britain or Singapore. How good Australian intelligence was has yet to investigated, but reports from Tokyo must have acknowledged invasion, because it was repeatedly under discussion.

Australians, complacent in the vast inland distances of their country had to reflect on the fact that history is littered with bad military decisions, like Hannibal crossing the Alps with unfortunate elephants, and Napoleon and Hitler's advances into Russia in winter. As Japanese forces advanced on Port Moresby in New Guinea, killing everyone in their path, the major Japanese base at Rabaul allowed Japanese forces to harass supply routes between the United States and Australia and New Zealand, as well as intimidate Australian civilians by their proximity.

John Curtin later said, 'An actual danger of invasion had never existed and the likelihood diminished through 1942 as allied victories eroded Japan's offensive capability'. The first part of that statement is questionable, the second is true.

In hindsight, the picture becomes more transparent, but not clear and in the 1940s, no-one in Australia could be certain of events because the Japanese themselves were indecisive. Australians discussed the news anxiously over endless cups of Bushells tea, trying to guess Japan's intentions so that they could safeguard the most precious beings in their lives - their children.

Would the first bombs be followed by the carpet bombing devastating Londoners, or three submarines in the Sydney Harbour followed by a fleet? Their house could be hit by a shell or bombed. The government's policy of calming the population with heavy censorship just made them more uneasy.

Chapter 3
Who's Telling the Truth?

Injured sailors from the Harbour were brought there after the sub raids. Within hours of their arrival all the staff would have known what had happened, and within a couple of days so would all their families and the whole street ... It really was foolish of the government to think it was 'keeping things quiet.

– Cassie Thornley

Chapter 3

The Japanese reached New Guinea and Indonesia. The enemy was on our doorstep. Everyone was uncomfortably aware our industry and population were around the coastline, many men were fighting overseas and refugees flooding in with tales of Japanese atrocities.

The weekly Darwin train arrived with mail and Chinese miners aboard. Well aware of the ferocity of the Japanese invasion of China in 1937, the miners fled to the safety of the hills. They were not waiting for official confirmation that a Japanese attack was imminent. Much of the confusion among the civilian population was caused by not knowing which authority was in charge, a case of the tail wagging the dog. The passenger lists of evacuees in the National Archives at Darwin show a chaotic record, with arrows, revisions and crossed out words.

Beatrice Yell tells about her two aunts, who were married to Dutch businessmen, working in Jakarta:

When the Japanese invaded in March 1942, so ending Dutch colonial rule, the two businessmen were arrested at work and sent to work, one on the Burma railway and one in the Japanese mines. The aunts, who had five young children between them, were given an hour to pack and be taken to a camp. They had no idea whether they would be away for a week or how long - never dreaming it would be for over three years. They packed two changes of clothes for everybody and one aunt took the youngest child's teddy bear and sewed her jewels inside it. She told the child never to part with the bear. In the camp, one Japanese guard fell for one of the aunts, who was blonde and graceful and wanted to install her in a house outside the camp with her children. She was tempted to comply, because it would mean more food for her children, and walked a fine line between keeping him interested and staying faithful to her husband, whom she loved very much, and hoped to be reunited with. She was able to ask the guard for information. He told her that Sydney and Melbourne had been bombed flat. He also said the aboriginals would be 'surplus to the needs of the Japanese'. The aunt believed him and thought that they must be better off in the camp in Indonesia than in Australia.

Although the food was scant, she carefully saved the rough sugar that they were allowed, in a jar, and when they were eventually allowed to leave and come to Australia, she was able to give the sugar to her weeping Australian relatives.

Some state government's position on home front security of 'wait and see' and 'it might never happen' statements to the Press reflected their uncertainty. Les Reedman's thoughts on the NSW government's plans:

I used to mow the lawn of Jack Frape, the Deputy Chief Inspector for Public Service Accommodation, and he told me that in case of invasion, the state government would retreat to Bathurst.

Apart from official evacuation from Queensland, no plans were made for civilians. The state governments were, however resigned to the possibility of invasion. War preparedness was happening in secret. The government had signed the *Official Secrets Act* for activities against the *Geneva Convention*. For instance, the Australian Department of Defence set up the Chemical Warfare Board in 1924 (later the Chemical Defence Board). An Australian Women's Army Servicewoman told me about mustard gas experiments in Proserpine in northern Queensland in 1943. She was told: 'Lieutenant Graham, we have a very important posting to offer you. It is strictly confidential and top secret. You will be the only woman officer and the station will be isolated. You will not be able to discuss it with your fellow officers or your family. You must have tact and patience. The girls must not talk about what is going on and you will have to censor every letter'. She was a marvellous woman. Her handsome, clever undergraduate husband returned traumatised from a Japanese work camp, never able to lead a normal life.

Since WWI, the military was obsessed with the idea of hydrogen cyanide being used in Australia. Japanese gas cylinders were found in New Guinea by the Australians as they advanced. Whether this gas was tested on troops is unclear.

Richard Featherstone-Haugh:

Dad had to go up to New Guinea. I saw him and my mother with their arms around each other, both crying. He picked me up and hugged me real hard. He came back, but he was not the same man and used to drink heavy. He would never take his trousers off or wear shorts on the beach and I found out that he had mustard gas burns from tests they did on the troops in New Guinea. My mother told me never to ask about it. He got a part pension. Later on, he was interviewed by Mike Willesee and after that he got a full pension with back payment.

About 16 types of highly unstable phosgene and mustard gas bombs from Britain were put in 14 storage depots, one a disused railway tunnel at Glenbrook. ICI had a contract for bleaching agents for contaminated ground. Mr P. Weldon went to England to study toxic gases and gasmasks which were to contain charred coconut shell filters (processed at the Colonial Sugar Refining Company at Pyrmont). Asbestos fibre mixed with merino wool was also suggested. British scientists in Townsville found mustard gas to be four times more effective in the tropics. As Curtin had promised 'a maximum of misery' in defeat, volunteers, some university students, arrived cheerfully to be used as guinea pigs. Hapless tethered goats exposed to the gas all died in great distress.

Australia's five wartime Prime Ministers, Robert Menzies, Arthur Fadden, John Curtin, Frank Forde and Ben Chifley employed censorship and propaganda. They would all have liked to present a grand plan for evacuation, but didn't have one. Flurries of committees were set up, ministers promising consideration of any scheme.

After a press release revealed details of Japanese naval positions during the Battle of the Coral Sea, Roosevelt ordered censorship in Australia. The Advisory War Council under Curtin granted GHQ censorship authority over the Australian Press. One result was that there was no mention of Australian troops from the middle of 1944 to January 1945.

Wartime governments, straddling Australia with censorship, propaganda and persecuting objectors, were perceived as withholding truth. Australians became deeply distrustful of published information, guessing at deletions. Postcards or letters from servicemen overseas had censor's thick pencils across them or sections cut out so stories flew about when a wounded man returned.

A Carefree War

As Pamela (Smith) Maddrell's father was a policeman he would have been aware of Manly Council trying to protect its civilians:

> Father was the station sergeant at Manly Police Station. He wanted us to go away, so we went to Goulburn from March to December 1942. There were Americans stationed nearby at North Head and he thought Manly might get cut off. There were trenches dug and sirens used to go off. Once we were in the pictures and a siren went off. We all had to get out and go into trenches. He was at the station a lot, sleeping there some nights. I knew a lot of children who were evacuated. We had two aunts and a grandmother living at Goulburn but my mother took me to a boarding house to stay and we visited them. I was 14, doing Intermediate at Goulburn High. We were looked after well at the boarding house where there were army wives and teachers - a nice rest for my mother - and I was happy. We got on with our lives. I studied music with a beautiful nun. We played tennis. I gradually made some friends. There was no phone at the boarding house, father visiting us once and sending letters and money by mail. The day I finished my Intermediate, I went to see *Fantasia*.

Lynton Bradford clearly saw enemy damage and wondered about the Press:

> I was ten and lived in Bronte in 1942. One morning we heard a report that a Japanese submarine off the coast had shelled Bondi and Woollahra but no harm had been done. I rode my bike over to Bondi, amazed to find the whole wall of the back room of a two storey brick house had gone and a large hole in the roadway. I can still see it now, a bed hanging precariously, sheets and curtains hanging over the edge. The hole in the roadway was huge and quite deep. The news report claimed no shell had exploded. How could all that damage result from an unexploded shell? I was then sent to live with my great aunt in Gerringong for a while, then to high school at Bathurst and Griffith until war's end.

Chapter 3

Geoff Potter described his grandmother, worried about her family, deciding to investigate things for herself after the attack:

> My gran, who lived in Mortlake on the Parramatta River, sent my uncle, then in his early teens, all the way over to Bondi the day after the attack, to see if other relatives were alright.

As part of the tactic to muzzle the Press, Prime Minister Menzies appointed widely criticised Keith Murdoch as Director General of Information on 8 June, 1940. *Smith's Weekly*, the lively broadsheet read around Australia since 1919, condemned the 'would-be Press and radio dictator'. *Smith's Weekly* was a patriotic magazine supporting diggers and aimed at the male market (especially returned servicemen). In contrast to dreary grey columns of newspaper print and smudgy half-tone pictures, *Smith's* readers enjoyed brash and funny illustrated cartoons, comic strips and sensational articles. The idea of easy-going individuals with a healthy disrespect for authority was central. One headline ran, 'A Censored Christmas', and warned Santa Claus to look out. On the serious side, the magazine supported the rights of returning soldiers and questioned prevailing attitudes towards shell shock. Started by Englishman Sir James Joynton Smith, other founders included Clyde Packer, father of Sir Frank Packer. *Smith's* didn't argue with authorities, it just went to print. Before the Japanese submarine attack in Sydney Harbour it showed a cartoon about a Japanese submarine caught in a fishing net, fishermen joking, 'It's undersize. Do you think we ought to throw it back?'

There had been a perception that a big bronzed Aussie would easily defeat the Japanese, seen as small and inferior, but as war progressed this was questioned.

Mary Moss:

> When Curtin became Prime Minister in October 1941 he made Beasley Minister for Supply and Development, (later Minister for Supply and Shipping), a vital portfolio in wartime. Beasley was a friend of my father's and I went to school with his daughter and he used to sometimes give us a ride in his Commonwealth car. In June 1942, when the Japanese submarines came into the Harbour,

we were going across the Sydney Harbour Bridge in Beasley's car, myself and two of his daughters. The air raid siren went off and the driver stopped the car. He walked away from it and looked over the side. He came back and said something quietly to Beasley who said to us in the back, 'Have you got your rosaries with you? Well you had better send up a prayer.' Apparently they had seen the periscope of a sub under the bridge and were petrified that we would be blown up.

True to policy control the *Daily Telegraph*, rather than reporting on page one subs prowling around the Harbour for ninety minutes before being spotted, described Princess Elizabeth at an informal dance, to save embarrassing the government and show up the smugly unprepared navy. This was the last straw for many parents who then sent their children away.

The Australian Government's Department of Information, one of seventeen departments from WWI, operated from 1939 to 1950 central to the role of government. *The National Security Act 1939* gave the government extraordinary powers over new regulations. Functioning in a democracy it was bitterly criticised. They minimised military forces being depleted, ships and planes obsolete, troops untrained and deployed overseas. In March 2015, men and women in the ADF numbered 56,000 with another 25,000 in reserves. They were supported by 20,600 public servants. The DMO had 7,000 military, civilian and contracted staff. The Department sought to calm the populace, cover governmental unpreparedness and understate reliance on the British in order to maintain morale. Propaganda created fear, vilified the enemy, dulled down defeats and emphasised victories, ensuring Australians accepted government proposals for their survival. Interestingly, the government never released a poster in lurid colours of a Japanese soldier advancing with a drawn bayonet. It was considered too confronting.

The Japanese were demonised with slogans: 'We've Always Despised Them - Now We Must Smash Them' and 'Every One a Killer'. General Tojo Hideki, wartime leader of Japan's government who died in 1948, with his close-cropped hair, moustache, and round spectacles, became a commonly caricatured member of the military dictatorship. Shrewd at bureaucratic infighting and fiercely partisan while army minister, he was an indecisive leader.

Australians looking to their government for guidance, understood the enemy was fearsome and barbaric, but were offered censored facts, and no solution to evacuation concerns, only empty reassurances.

An example of censored reporting is the bombing of Darwin, false impressions of which linger. A typical report in the *Melbourne Argus*, 21 February, 1941: '... In two air raids on Darwin yesterday, it is believed that the total casualties were 17 killed and 24 wounded. Nine of the civilian fatalities were members of the Darwin Post Office Staff, including the postmaster, his wife and daughter. Latest information received at RAAF headquarters indicates that in yesterday's raids no vital damage was done to RAAF installations'. The National Archives currently states 243 people died, with up to 400 casualties. Tokyo radio propaganda reported Darwin as bombed and left in flames. With hindsight, we know the attack on Darwin was not a precursor to an invasion. The Japanese were preparing to invade Timor. An air attack was to hinder Darwin's potential as an allied base and damage morale. But nobody knew those details until much later.

Bill Willett realised that civilians were uninformed:

> The government shut down information on the Darwin bombing, there were more bombs dropped there than on Pearl Harbour, but most Australians didn't know.

The Advertiser, Adelaide, 28 February, 1942, carried a description of the journey of 300 evacuees from Darwin. 'After a trip described as a 'nightmare' nearly 300 men, women, and children evacuees, many of them wearing the only clothes they possess, completed a 2,000-mile journey from Darwin. Some who were slightly wounded in the raid carried out by the Japanese were among the arrivals. The more seriously wounded were kept at military hospitals for attention at Alice Springs and other northern centres. Some of the men had no shoes, while others arrived clad in shorts and singlets only. One man said he left Darwin with only a pair of shorts. Good Samaritans had given him a shirt and hat at Katherine'.

Other towns bombed included Townsville, Wyndham, Derby, Broome, Port Hedland and Katherine. Australians were mostly unaware of these bombings. Farmers watched as nine 'Betty' bombers from the Japanese Navy's Tokao Kokutai, 23rd Koku Sentai circled over Katherine at 12.20 pm, disappeared and returned to drop about ninety-one, 60 kg bombs. Eighty-four of these bombs were anti-personnel 'Daisy Cutters', falling on the almost deserted Katherine airfield. Some aboriginal people were unfortunately killed. Outside the loss of life damage was minimal. With The Advisory War Council controlling Press statements, Australians failed to grasp the gravity of attacks, either minimising them in comparison with the London Blitz, or unaware of what had really happened.

Allied naval and merchant ships were sunk off Australia's coast by Japanese submarines and mine laying German surface raiders, one being the auxiliary cruiser *Pinquin* and another, the *Kormoran* which sank HMAS *Sydney*. Many losses were hushed up but the HMAS *Sydney* was a high profile loss. A fund was started immediately and a new ship commissioned with the same name. The following poem from the *Western Mail,* 10 December, 1942 is from David Beeves, aged 13:

HMAS Sydney
Out roar the bombers, but oh! too late
To save our ship from her wicked fate
So home they go - the commanders to tell
What fate the two ships befell?
But that ship that has long swept the sea,
Will never die down in history.
So every penny we can, we must save,
To replace that cruiser that sank to her grave.

Journalists complained about censorship. The Department of Information issued an average of eight instructions daily on top of General Macarthur's communiqués. In a later article in *Time Magazine* 1951, these communiqués were called 'a total farce' and 'Alice-in-Wonderland information, handed out at high level'. Newspapers, 60% of their pre-war size, indicated to readers the extent of deletions with blank spaces, as journalists struggled to write stories. This breached the *National Security Regulations* so police stopped distribution. But the government could not stop people talking. Cassie Thornley worked for some years on the archives at Sydney Hospital:

> Injured sailors from the Harbour were brought there after the sub raids. Within hours of their arrival all the staff would have known what had happened, and within a couple of days so would all their families and the whole street etc. It really was foolish of the government to think it was 'keeping things quiet - imagine how the story would have grown by the end of the street!

Australia's defence strategy of merged British and Australian navies retaining control of her seas had crumpled. With inaction for civilian safety came heavy censorship with 'Keep Calm and Carry On' and 'Stay Put and Sit Tight' the order of the day.

Civilians and groups like The Teacher's Federation pressed the government for civilian strategies. The federal government first stated in February 1942, at a meeting of the War Council and Premiers, '... large scale evacuation of the civilian population would be detrimental to the morale of the people and should be strongly discouraged, both in the interests of the public and of production, but it was realised that limited evacuation of areas contiguous to possible targets and the removal of young children from certain congested city areas might be considered necessary'. It would impose on state and federal governments a tremendous burden and '...in other countries when families were broken up by evacuation, the efficiency of the worker who remained behind was considerably impaired'. Councils, which had been delegated responsibilities agreed wholeheartedly. When people quietly started moving their children away from perceived danger government gave a sigh of relief and offered free train travel to accompanying adults.

Donald Dunkley quoted in Peter Grose's *A Very Rude Awakening*: 'A lot of families were ready to go to relatives up in the country. If an invasion actually did take place, we had some relatives living in Harden, the Riverina part of New South Wales. We were advised to contact relatives in the country and see if they were willing to take us if we had to evacuate. They said yes, by all means, we're happy to take you. So, had there been an invasion, I don't know how on earth we would have got there, but we did have this place earmarked that we could have gone to. I think a lot of other families around the place had relatives in the country, and they were all ready to go if necessary'.

There were whole streets where nobody moved for various reasons, but elsewhere convoys of women got together taking away busloads of children. If there had been an unplanned evacuation, imagine the chaos of choked roads and violence at railway stations, wharves, and airports. Cinemas had shown nightmare processions of dispossessed families in Europe with possessions heaped on anything with wheels, lost children, dogs straggling miserably behind, getting strafed and bombed. But of course it couldn't happen here!

Voluntary evacuation happened from Burnie, Tasmania to Bourke NSW, but north of the so-called Brisbane Line was enforced by state governments. During early 1942, Northern Queensland schools and mission stations were officially evacuated with the SS *Ormiston* used for compulsory evacuation of civilians from Thursday, Horn and Hammond Islands in the Torres Strait. European, Chinese and Islander women and children were sent to Cairns, Townsville and Brisbane. (Other coastal vessels used in the evacuation of North Queensland civilians included the SS *Katoomba, Taroona* and *Wandana*).

In Cairns, 4,000 women and children moved to safer places in the country assisted by the State Government voluntary evacuation scheme. A request was made to the State Government to upgrade the road from Cardwell to Kirrama in February 1942.

NSW Bureaucrats tried to take over the evacuation movement generated from ground level. On 17 January, 1942 Mr Heffron, Minister for National Emergency Services: 'Public schools reopen at 9 am on the following Thursday in Sydney, Wollongong, Port Kembla area for parents to register their children for voluntary evacuation on supplied forms'. There was an issue with striking teachers. The Teacher's Federation said that the issuing of the forms did not mean teachers should take it as an instruction that they were to return to duty that day...

Chapter 3

Following the issue of forms, there was criticism about government plans. Parents asked what financial obligation were they under to pay for their children's evacuation? Was it intended to move children in school units? Would children in the same family be kept together? Could their mothers accompany them? How will the mothers be accommodated? What kind of accommodation would there be? How much notice would families be given? What clothing and equipment would they need to take? So many questions.

Under-Secretary for Labour and Industry, Mr Bellemore assured mothers unable voluntarily to send their children into the country that a plan was being developed: 'If such an emergency occurs it is hoped to evacuate people in family units and adopt the escort system for those children, who would travel to safer areas unaccompanied by their parents. The Education Department should build up educational facilities in those country districts'.

In January 1942 all NSW state schools opened but only 12% of parents registered for voluntary evacuation. Newtown Council called for compulsory registration for evacuation, food control in an emergency, household registration for NES and manpower.

Whilst the NSW government waffled and dithered, making empty promises and denying there was a possible disaster about to happen, strict regulations were issued from Canberra about safeguarding the wellbeing of refugee British children. The Commonwealth Minister for the Interior became the guardian of every overseas child upon arrival in Australia until the child reached 21 years-of-age, left Australia or the regulation ceased to apply. Custodians of the children were prevented from in any way demanding remuneration from the parents. The duties and responsibilities were monitored. State authorities had to keep a register of both custodians and children allotted to them with all the relevant particulars. Custodians were required to notify the authorities of change of address and were forbidden to leave the State without permission from the authorities. If a child absconded, became ill, had an accident or died, the authorities had to be informed. A custodian had to satisfy authorities that they were suitable persons and this approval could be revoked at any time. These regulations only applied to the children placed under an agreement between the Commonwealth and British governments. The Australian children who were evacuated were outside any regulation. Parents, usually mothers, made individual decisions and were helped by having subsidised train fares but there was no monitoring of their situation. Luckily, evacuees seem to have come through the experience unscathed.

Positive propaganda was practised by all sides. On the Australian home front, everything was war related, so housewives shopping, children collecting waste materials, older people making camouflage nets and young boys drilling all felt included, useful and productive in the war effort. Bruce Whitefield remembers:

> Men too old for the army used to practice throwing hand-grenades at the football ground - although no actual grenades were thrown just short lengths of water pipes.

Pairs of socks with little handwritten notes for example, 'God bless you soldier boy. From Melissa aged 11', were welcomed by soldiers. The 'Children's Corner' in newspapers was filled with heroic war poems.

On the Japanese home front, mothers of kamikaze pilots embroidered their *hachimaki* or headbands with inspirational motifs. In war-themed *Kamishibai,* or 'paper plays', street performers used *Emakimono* or 'picture scrolls' to convey stories.

Entertainers kept troops and civilians happy. American servicemen taught Australian girls to jitterbug at the Trocadero. The United Services Organisation (USO) established in January 1942 by the Americans brought entertainment to frontline troops with stars like John Wayne, Joe E Brown, Jerry Colonna, Al Johnson, Gary Cooper, Jack Benny and Bob Hope. The Australian Military established the 1st Australian Entertainment Unit, giving more than 12,000 performances, with stars like George Wallace, Michael Pate, Gladys Moncrieff, and Jenny Howard.

Anybody looking different or with an unusual surname was eyed by their neighbours. Jim Altman, who went to Killara when it was still largely bush:

> My parents were refugees from Europe and arrived in Australia in 1939. They rented a place in Neutral Bay, near the water. The

Japanese came into the Harbour and it was clear that the Harbour Bridge would be a target. My parents left Neutral Bay and bought a place along a dirt road in the outlying suburbs –in Killara – we are still there. There was a dairy farm, so we had fresh milk and cream. The rest of it was bush. My parents were classed as enemy aliens because they came from Vienna and had passports stamped by Nazi Germany authorities, so they were not allowed a radio, in case they were spies. One day, I saw some children playing in the road with a radio and I was really frightened of the radio and ran home crying and crying - it seemed to me such a dangerous thing. I was terrified.

Short wave radio ownership was viewed with suspicion. Toowoomba RSL urged the government to seize all civilian radios, so fifth columnists could not use them. Radios, now in 80% of households were a key source of news. Anthony Euwer:

Around this time, we got a series of wireless sets delivered on appro, and there was a lot of thumb-sucking done while a decision was made to finally buy a small brown bakelite model which sat on the sideboard and was plugged into the 'other' power point. (There was one in the sunroom which mum used for the iron). It then became the show piece for the neighbours, as they visited our house to view this magic extravagance. I used to come home from school for lunch and listen to *Blue Hills*.

James R Young writing from Japan for the *Sunday Times*, 5 April, 1942:

The radio war proved a tame affair in 1939-45. We'd expect such an international blast and counterblast of news and views that a twirl of the dial would give us all sorts of exciting slants on current history. It proved quite the contrary. The enemy's news-in-English was so wildly improbable, or such a dull repetition of somebody else's communiqués, that we soon tired of it. In other words we knew in advance what other nations were thinking, or being told to think, or telling us to think.

Much to the distress of many with relatives and friends in Britain, BBC broadcasts were reduced. Japanese propaganda through their radio broadcasts claimed they wanted to help Australia break free of Britain and America. Australians and Allies in Europe heard Lord Haw ranting, and Allies in the Pacific every day at 8pm, heard the lilting voice of Tokyo Rose, beamed from powerful radio transmitters in Japan, over the Aleutians and South Pacific, taunting servicemen over the loss of American ships, in reality the reports where often uncannily correct. Once they informed listeners that Japanese troops would shortly be landing at Brice Henry's private aerodrome at Riversdale. Prime Minister Lyons and his wife had landed there once to inspect a cattle scheme - was that the source of their intelligence? The Japanese dropped propaganda pamphlets showing American servicemen with Australian servicemen's wives.

The Australian Government dealt with conscientious objectors, who would appear before a Military Exemptions Court, with no right of appeal, their names and addresses published in the Press. There is a humorous side to the court hearings which were usually held before a Brigadier. Jehovah's Witness members objected to killing. One said '... they were still in a temporal world, and while they were doing that, they would rather, until Armageddon came, be under British rule than Nazi rule'. Another said he would reason with an invading Japanese soldier intending to assault his wife or daughter. 'Ha,' said the Brigadier triumphantly, 'but you don't speak Japanese!' Some objectors joined the anti-war Christadelphians, but after admitting they had only 'seen the light' in January 1942, were dismissed as not being serious. From 1 November, 1941 to 31 March, 1942, only ten cases were exempt completely from military training and 75 were exempt from military service but directed elsewhere. Many Australians did not realise there were 1,000 prosecutions, some accused persons of both genders, and children, imprisoned for six months, some interned until war's end. The Communist Party was banned and members of Australia First Movement (which never had more than 65 members) interned for opposition to the war.

Healthy men who did not join up were social outcasts. Engineered patriotic feelings of the day could be very destructive. Valda (Dundas) McDonald remembers a haven of peace for her and her mother at

Werris Creek in the tragic pressures that war brings:

> I was born in March 1939 and lived at Maroubra with my parents. In 1941 my mother took me up to Werris Creek to my grandparents. They treated me beautifully and were so kind. My father was a bus driver. My mother told him that if he joined up she wouldn't be there for him to come home to. It was emotional blackmail really. He had white feathers put in his pockets and paint daubed on his back. It caused a lot of unhappiness in the home. What made it worse was that his younger brother was killed at Sandakan. Dad suffered a lot at not being a 'returned man'.

Newsreels with robust music backing showed energised soldiers gaining positions. Damien Parer a well known war photographer and cameraman complained about the censorship of his brilliant footage. The reality of the war he had filmed, diluted or altered to match the government's message.

The purpose of propaganda was to feed civilians with images of an inhuman enemy, to maintain patriotic enthusiasm and to calm and reassure people and keep order. The words of *The Pearce Report* at the outbreak of war, was music to the ears of the Australian government, declaring: '…the situation demands government action, the public are eagerly awaiting it and the time is ripe for general sacrifice by the community.'

The *Daily Telegraph*, Monday, July 21, 1941:

It must not be forgotten that the Japanese have an immutable policy. The word immutable is their own. Their immutable line is known to everybody for it is simply the aspiration to control that undefined place called "Greater East Australia". The Japanese may dart here and dart there, but they are always trying to get East Asia under their exclusive control. The Japanese Minister to Australia, Mr Kawai, says in his book *Goal of Japanese Expansionism* that 'this is in accord with a mysterious force of nature called 'Misubi' and that it will result in the beautification and sublimification of Asiatic life. But the Chinese, Americans and Australians seem to doubt this.

A Carefree War

It has been suggested that Curtin played up the threat of invasion through 1942-43 to win the August 1943 election, knowing from secret documents the Japanese did not intend to invade. But there is room for doubt. Why did the Japanese print Occupation Money, which could have been used in Australia? The Japanese produced Occupation Money in a variety of notes such as Guilders, Pesos, Dollars and Pounds. It is assumed that their Pound notes were probably for use in the British Islands of the Pacific Ocean (not including Australia) and adjacent seas, including New Guinea, rather than as part of a 'planned occupation' of Australia.

When on 5 August, 1944, Japanese prisoners of war housed at Cowra, New South Wales staged a breakout, resulting in the death of 231 Japanese prisoners with a further 108 wounded, Australians were aghast. Four Australians, Privates Hardy, Jones and Shepherd were killed and Lieutenant Doncaster was killed when ambushed during the recapture. It was shocking to hear of dead Japanese soldiers strewn around railway tracks and hanging from trees.

In desperation, Australian mothers found ways to evacuate their children or to get a job in the country. They continually asked themselves and their friends and relatives *if* there was going to be an invasion, *when* it would happen and *where*. Everywhere was alive with rumours. They already knew the record of the Japanese Imperial Army. Those who could do so fled.

Chapter 4
Call to Action

... there will still be Australians fighting on Australian soil until the turning point be reached, and we will advance over blackened ruins, through blasted and fire-swept cities, across scorched plains, until we drive the enemy into the sea.

– Prime Minister Curtin in a radio broadcast, 14 March, 1942

A Carefree War

We were told to 'give till it hurts'. Civilians were reassured by 'doing their bit'. The Children's Aluminium Army scrounged bits of scrap metal. The Principal of Shore School, North Sydney berated pupils in the school magazine for only producing 177 camouflage nets in 1942. Children spent evenings and weekends growing vegetables, selling mountains of sausage rolls and scones made by Tuck Shop Ladies to buy material and wool to make balaclava helmets, mittens and pullovers to send overseas. There were many appeals and funds to choose from and gifts and donations went to Darwin, Alice Springs and Milne Bay. Children's vocabulary expanded: 'prang' for crash, 'blue' for a fight. 'Perspex' was the new glass for plane windows. Children scrounged empty machine gun cartridges to make rings from, stole cartridges and played with war detritus. They begged apple jelly jam and chocolate from the troops.

Although in 1941 there was political speculation about the actual timing of the outbreak of war, at the end of August 1941, Permanent Military Forces in Australia numbered only 5,025 with 12,915 in garrison battalions and 43,720 in the Volunteer Defence Corps. The Government issued its 'call to action' on 21 March, 1942: 'There are no more parties: Mr Curtin is Australia's leader. There are no rights worth a damn until we have beaten the Japanese. The time has come to stop prating about our rights, money, privileges, profits or anything else. We know well enough how conquered countries are treated. Australians need to put themselves first'.

Society was in turmoil, with women alone and now having to make far-reaching decisions that could impact their families' safety. The Japanese invaded New Guinea and about 1,700 adults were evacuated from Port Moresby to Cairns. NF 388965 Campbell, Elsie heard the news on a radio crackling with static whilst working on a Congregationalist mission station on an island called Kwato near Samurai.

I came to Sydney with about 500 women on the Neptune. In Sydney, friends advised me that the Army was seeking personnel. With two brothers in the services, enlisting in the Australian Women's Army Service seemed the logical thing to do and I was soon on the first training course at Killara.

Chapter 4

Elsie was just one woman pressing reluctant authorities now forced to recognize womanpower. Women did not want to sit at home and stare at the three plaster flying ducks on their lounge room wall. A sense of urgency coupled with the British example led to 'The Formation and Control of an Australian Women's Army Service to release men for military duties for employment with fighting units', signed by Mr Forde, Minister for the Army, in 1942. Women would be paid less, and not taught to shoot – but of course they could. Many women in the country areas, who shot rabbits for the pot during the 1930s Depression, joined vigilante groups and were handy with a gun if an unwanted intruder appeared. Society's appraisal of women's role was being challenged. If an army 'rookie' found herself 'in the family way', whether married or not, there was an order hastily written for the *Care and Disposal of Pregnant Women*.

The Japanese threat brought about a spectacular growth in all the women's services. By mid-1943, there were 8,000 nurses, 16,000 WAAFs, 14,000 WRANS, 2,000 Land Army girls and 18,000 AWAS. The initial reluctance to let women 'do their bit' quickly changed to admiration.

Elaine Thomas was upset at the news of the hostilities:

> My brother and I learned of the outbreak of war while coming home from church. I started to cry and he told me not to be silly – he could see it was about to happen. He was already in the militia, training at weekends at age sixteen. He lied about his age and joined the AIF. I stayed at school until I was sixteen but I couldn't concentrate knowing that I could be working – there were six children younger than me and a terrible war on.

The services demanded more and more women to train. They went into industry. They were tram conductors, and - shock, horror - they were wearing trousers! The Women's Land Army kept up production on the farms.

Women and were in the war effort, but what would happen to the children in case of invasion?

On 29 September, 1939, the *Sydney Morning Herald* wrote: 'Minister for Education, Mr Drummond said that since the crisis of September 1938, the government had appointed an expert officer of the Department, who had had experience of wartime conditions, to make a survey of the areas which might have to be evacuated in the event of attack and the places to which children might have to be transferred. Steps had also been taken to find out the extent to which evacuated children could be lodged at homes in safe areas. Mr Drummond emphasized that the military authorities considered the possibility of air attacks on Australia remote and that it was not necessary to provide shelters in Sydney like those in Great Britain.

The Minister for National Emergency Services, Mr Heffron, addressing the Teachers' Federation 23 December, 1941, said: '...on the subject of the evacuation of children, people were now wanting things done in a great hurry.' Previously, when he had wanted things done in a great hurry he had been regarded as an alarmist. 'We still hope that the real thing will not reach Australia,' Mr Heffron said, 'but if it does we shall be better prepared because of what has been done already.'

Friday, 6 February, 1942, *Sydney Morning Herald* editorial:

... decisions regarding evacuation and kindred matters which the War Council and State Premiers reached on Wednesday show a praiseworthy grasp of realities, and it is to be hoped that they will be carefully studied by the public, which has for a considerable time been bewildered by conflicting statements from official sources. While any large-scale evacuation is rightly discouraged, limited evacuation from 'target areas' is recommended, and the suggestion that safer parts of specific cities rather than more distant places should be chosen is wise. There should now be no delay in announcing the target areas so that people who reside in them may take whatever steps they think advisable for their protection ...

Chapter 5
What is Really Happening?

*... any large scale evacuation at the present time will be
ill-advised and contrary to the best interests of the country.*

– Town Clerk's Office, Sydney, February 1942

A Carefree War

The Allies did not consider Australia at risk, The British Admiralty appearing under the impression Japan was too involved with China to be a threat. Churchill advised the Australian War Cabinet as late as August 1940, that in the event of a Japanese invasion of Australia, '… we would then cut our losses in the Mediterranean and sacrifice every interest, except only the defence and feeding of this Island, on which all depends, and would proceed in good time to your aid …'

Geoffrey Brooke in his book, *Singapore's Dunkirk*, says on page seven: When Churchill was on his way to meet Roosevelt at Placentia Bay in August 1941 and was asked whether he thought the Japanese would attack Malaya, he replied, 'No I don't think so. And if they do, they will find they have bitten off more than they could chew'.

Australian civilians had their invasion fears fuelled by obvious signs of war as they went about their daily lives. Refugees arrived constantly. In December 1941, five hundred women were hastily evacuated from Salamaua, leaving half prepared Christmas cakes and puddings in their kitchens. They arrived in a very distressed state in Cairns to tell their stories.

On Friday, 13 March, 1942, Commander-in-Chief, Vice-Admiral Sir Geoffrey Layton, issued the following statement: In view of the present unsettled state and the problems of food supply, all persons not normally resident in Ceylon, who are not employed on essential war work, must arrange to leave as soon as passages are available. This includes the wives and children of naval, air force and military personnel, also non-Ceylonese women residents with young children. Gillian Branagan was one of these children, evacuated twice:

> My sister was evacuated from Canonbury hospital, Darling Point to Fairbridge Farm, Molong. My mother and I took a house there for a year and visited the farm on weekends in a horse-drawn sulky. I think it was 1941. This was a steep learning curve for my mother as we'd come from Ceylon where she'd had servants.

Chapter 5

In New South Wales, pressure was put on the authorities.

HON WJ McKELL

PREMIER NEW SOUTH WALES

CANBERRA

RESPONDING TO REQUISITION HAVE CONVENED
PUBLIC MEETING TOWN HALL EIGHT O CLOCK
THURSDAY NIGHT FIFTH INSTANT STOP MY
OPINION IMPERATIVE PREMIER OR HIS ACCREDITED
REPRESENTATIVE ATTEND TO BE FIRST SPEAKER TO
EXPLAIN STATE PLAN EVACUATION ALLAY PUBLIC
UNREST MANIFEST STOP EXPLANATION IN BROAD
PRINCIPLES GOVERNMENTS PROPOSALS ESSENTIAL
FOR PRESERVATION PUBLIC MORALE OWING
TO ABSENCE OF INFORMATION OF AUTHENTIC
CHARACTER ANY EXISTENT CONSIDERED
PLAN STOP

CRICK

LORD MAYOR SYDNEY - WIRE SENT 4/2/42

This meeting was largely in response to a letter from The Teachers'
Federation, who were continually vocal about evacuation and the
continuing education of displaced children. On 29 January, 1942, they
had sent the following to Stanley Crick, the Lord Mayor of Sydney:

Dear Sir,

*We the following citizens of this city request you to call a public meeting
on Thursday February 5, 1942, at 8 pm for the purpose of considering
the question of evacuation of civilians from vulnerable areas, yours
faithfully ... The following signatures included The Federation
President and 16 administrative members and 18 signatures from
Phillip Street, (probably lawyers).*

The bureaucrats appeared bereft of ideas about evacuation, but nervous
about the situation, as is shown by the telegram above, a speedy request
(29 January was a Thursday) to the citizen's demands.

From the Town Clerk's Office, Sydney, February 1942:

'... any large scale evacuation at the present time will be ill-advised and contrary to the best interests of the country.'

'Let us, too,' ran the editorial in the *Riverina Advertiser* on Friday, 30 January, 1942, 'direct a little constructive criticism ... against those who have charge of evacuation arrangements, or lack of them. By this time, the state government in close cooperation with the Federation authorities should have had everything in readiness, all arrangements complete for a smooth, quick evacuation of women and children inland and others away from the coastal areas. But is there any such plan? There is not. If anything happened tomorrow, I can visualise the disorder, chaos and panic which would result. No-one knows where to go, how to get there or what to do.'

Meanwhile, all over Australia, small groups of people went into action. 'Following on recent activities in connection with the proposed evacuation scheme of soldier's wives and children to this district,' writes the *Murrumburrah Signal*, we have to report that the 2/1st Pioneer Battalion Comforts Fund committee have new finalised arrangements for the taking over of the Carrington and Doncaster Hotels at Harden, and the Commercial Hotel at Murrumburrah. Mrs. O'Malley Wood (President) together with several members of her committee arrived in Harden on Wednesday morning and a small number of evacuees were accommodated the same afternoon. A further party of approximately 170 evacuees will arrive today (Friday) and during next week an additional 200 will be accommodated. The evacuees will bring all their personal belongings, bed linen, blankets, and cutlery. Families will be kept together as far as possible. The rooms at the Carrington Hotel will be turned into dormitories for boys. The cooking will be done by the mothers on a roster system under the supervision of two head cooks. The evacuees will have their own entrance to the hotel, which will carry on its bar business as usual'.

'Moree will give a warm welcome to as many families as the town can accommodate,' said a Mr Cavanagh. 'Many of the mothers I have interviewed have to complete their affairs before they can leave Sydney, but it is expected that family groups will be sent from the city all next week. Half a dozen families left on yesterday's train.'

Chapter 5

The Editorial in the *Australian Women's Weekly*, 27 December, 1941 was entitled, 'If the children must go away'. It ran in part, 'When the mothers of England had to send their children into the country for safety, a sigh of sympathy ran round the globe. The going away of the children was the greatest heartache of all, and Australian mothers, as they sang their children to sleep, thanked God they had been spared that. Now they are facing the same heartache themselves. From many of the danger points, parents have already sent their youngsters to relatives or friends in safer districts. In several states, authorities are finalising their plans to evacuate youngsters from threatened areas. Some mothers have been able to go with their children ... these are the lucky ones. The others face as sad a parting as life can hold.' The article called on parents to steel themselves if the authorities demand evacuation.

In New South Wales, there was a flurry of activity, most of which seems to have been a delegation process. The Federal government delegated to the state governments, who delegated to councils. Councils consulted with bodies like the National Emergency Services and further delegated tasks and held meetings. In the metropolitan area, it was decided rest, emergency, feeding centres and local depots for food, clothing and general supplies, would be set up and a central control would survey the population to determine how many may need to be evacuated and which houses could be requisitioned for bomb victims or those fleeing danger spots. Evacuation registers were set up with cards for each household. Looking through the cards for western Sydney, which requested full names, gender, age, religion, occupation and state of health, a picture of overcrowding and poor health emerges along with unwillingness to open their doors. 'No spare floor space,' was often scribbled on the cards.

In Sydney, armbands and windscreen stickers, red with 'EV' stenciled in black were made available to authorised personnel. The President, Mayor, and Town Clerk said they all wanted one.

Cigarette cards dwindled and died because of paper supplies. Just prior to the war, children collected many with war themes. Besides the different ships, tanks, weapons, and regiments, there were civilian themes: Choosing your Refuge Room, Rendering Your Refuge Room Gas-Proof, Making a Door Gas-Proof, Window Protection, Window Protection Against Blast, Types of Splinter-Proof Wall, Protecting Your Windows - A Sandbag Defence, Equipping your Refuge Room, Equipping Your Refuge Room, A Garden Dug-Out, Incendiary Bomb and its Effect, Incendiary Bomb Cooling Down, and so on.

A partial blackout, called by some a brownout was ordered by the government in New South Wales from July to December 1941. Advertising and floodlights were banned, shop windows and display boards darkened. Outside lights were forbidden on homes and wardens tapped on doors and windows at telltale chinks of light. There were no night time sports fixtures. Older Australians knew pasting strips of brown paper across glass helped in a bomb blast. Cars crept along with slatted and hooded headlights, white stripes painted along their sides. No maps or forecasts were given. *The Land* urged its readers to use a rainfall registration chart for 1942, provided free for its readers, because of the Government's decision to restrict the publication of weather information and rainfall details. Restrictions on weather information were taken for security reasons after the outbreak of war with Japan, because it could aid the enemy. Farmers could keep their own record for farming purposes.

School children bought War Savings Certificates and Treasury notes from five shillings upwards. You could not ignore the signs of war, picking your way through sandbagged public buildings, riding on camouflaged buses, and seeing coastline gun batteries and observation posts. You dug your own backyard shelter.

Bev Kingston and her family remained staunchly behind as their friends and neighbours left:

We sat it out in Manly, me and Mum under the dining room table, Mum said there were too many spiders in the air raid shelter.

Cliffs and beautiful beaches had a menacing air, with rolls of barbed wire and anti-tank devices, a large metal gate pulled back daily to allow people onto the beach. Some parents were frightened of mines and would not let their children on beaches.

Chapter 5

Kate Riseley, Archivist, Shore School, North Sydney:

> One of the boys who was evacuated, Jim Creer, was on weekend leave one time and was staying at a hotel in North Sydney. That night he had to evacuate the hotel because it was struck by bullets from a Japanese submarine!

The newspapers were full of fifth column activity. September 1945, *Adelaide News:*

> Japanese plans to land troops in Australia may have been based on information sent by a Japanese spy who before the war stayed at a Brisbane hotel. That is the opinion of some of Australia's best secret service agents. The Jap's spying tour through Queensland became known to the secret service because of the astuteness of a chambermaid at the hotel in which the Jap stayed. The chambermaid had been cleaning the spy's room when she overturned a big case. It was unlocked and from it spilled hundreds of pictures. She glanced at a few of the markings, and phoned what was then the equivalent of the war time security service. A detective made quick plans and before the Jap had returned to his room that night photographic copies had been taken of all his documents and pictures. Landing spots important among these were his surveys and notes on the Iron Range area of Cape York Peninsula. Landing spots, routes, water supplies, and other facilities were noted. When the Allied fleets beat back the Japanese naval force in the Coral Sea battle of 1942, the Japanese were only 150 miles off this stretch.

New York Federal agents made two raids near New York, in March 1942, breaking a spy ring, directing Axis submarines to ships along the North Atlantic coast. They arrested 52 residents of a German seaman's home in Hoboken, New Jersey, seizing short-wave radios and wireless transmission sets. A Federal Bureau of Investigation official said, 'We regard the Hoboken round-up as one of the most important yet made.' Civilians became familiar with the demands of rationing, butter and household linen from 6 June, 1943, meat from 17 January, 1944, clothing ration card May 1942. Tea was in short supply.

A Carefree War

Mary Moss:

> We ate well in the country, but it was not good in the cities. I remember when I started nursing in 1949; we still had rationing for butter, sugar and tea. I had to give my ration book to the hospital and mother was annoyed because I spent a day and a half at home and she didn't have my coupons.

In between the war effort and air raid drills, people sat around kitchen tables in the blackout, planning how to protect their children. 'Sit down, I'll put the kettle on,' was said reassuringly while they made plans to evacuate and so began a most remarkable and widespread voluntary evacuation phenomenon, which in all states below the Brisbane Line came from the people with little official help or guidance apart from a belated offers from the government of lists of what to take and free railway tickets.

By June 1940, the Britain stood alone against Germany. Menzies called for an 'all in war effort' and with the support of Curtin, amended the *National Security Act,* extending government powers to tax, acquire property, control businesses and the labour force and allow for conscription of men for the 'defence of Australia'.

The Japanese advanced relentlessly up the Malay Peninsula, with most able bodied Australian men overseas. In March 1942, General Douglas MacArthur was appointed Supreme Commander of Allied Forces in the South-West Pacific. Australia looked to America for defence.

The RMS *Queen Mary* became known as the *'Grey Ghost'* during the war. Her departure from Sydney was supposed to be secret. (Keeping the whereabouts of a ship over 80,000 tons, laden with troops would be a bit of a challenge). These were the brave young boys going to fight for the Empire, truth and justice. However, women waving goodbye walked back to empty houses, painfully aware that their men were not at home to defend them.

The NSW government's position towards civilians was succinctly expressed by John Curtin, March 14, 1942: 'Out of every ten men in Australia four are wholly engaged in war as members of the fighting forces or making the munitions and equipment to fight with. The other six, besides feeding and clothing the whole ten and their families, have to produce the food and wool and metals which Britain needs for her very existence.' Australia's industrial and human resources had become wholly focused on supporting the allies with money, armaments, troops, wool, skins and meat.

The NSW Premier, Mr McKell:

Australia's war efforts had been based on the assumption that battles would be fought far from her own territory. The pick of the fighting men were sent overseas and industrially Australia had concentrated on organising a vast machine which would equip not only her own troops but other Empire forces. Only the very little that could be spared was diverted to building up air and civil defence organisations at home.

In Germany, on Thursday, 3 June, 1943 in *Das Reich*, a sad dirge ran:

Under the plan, not only people whose homes have been destroyed will be shifted, but practically the entire civilian population except armament workers. Civilians in Westphalia will be moved gradually to Bavaria, and residents of Berlin will be sent to Pomerania, East Prussia, and the provinces of Brandenburg. Preparations are already nearly completed for evacuating all school children from Duisburg. Eighteen thousand children have left Hamburg.

Curtin's government made it clear to Churchill, in a series of secret cables that the 6th, 7th and 9th Divisions, sent to the Middle East under the Menzies government must return home for the defence of Australia. First home was the 6th Division. The 7th was all back by May 1942, the 9th by May 1943. A group of Australian Women's Army Service wrote home about the reassuring sight of the *Queen Mary*, the *Aquitania*, the *Isle de France* and the *Empress of Bermuda* bringing the 9th Division home, as they were walking to Bellevue Hill on a rest day from Victoria Barracks. As the men came on shore, the *Australian Women's Weekly* ran stories of emotional reunions between wives and husbands, sweethearts, fathers, mothers and sons, sons and daughters. It didn't matter what shape the men were in as long as the family was together again.

Chapter 6

Getting the Children Away

What are we going to do about the children? ... Now, when Australia is in imminent danger, hundreds and thousands of parents are thinking mainly of one problem- the safety of their youngsters ...

– The *Australian Women's Weekly*, 27 December, 1941.

Chapter 6

Australia, a land of immigrants was largely caught up in the turmoil overseas, wondering about friends and relatives.

Cassie Thornley:

> Every evening, in 1938, silence fell for the 7 pm news. In summer, over tea, and in winter in the lounge by the fire we had to sit quietly while Tom listened with a far-away look as he tracked the latest bombing raids and thought of his family remaining in Austria.

The *Australian Women's Weekly* 27 December, 1941, 'In every coastal city in Australia this last fortnight, one question has run like a refrain through the news and rumours of war. It is: What are we going to do about the children? Ever since Europe felt the full horror of aerial warfare, the plight of children has aroused the indignation of men and women. Now, when Australia is in imminent danger, hundreds and thousands of parents are thinking mainly of one problem - the safety of their youngsters,'

Councils had interminable meetings about evacuation, mostly deciding there was no future in voluntary evacuation, that it must be funded and compulsory. But how would they enforce it?

Bruce Baskerville tells a sad story of confusion at Geraldton, West Australia:

> On the 31st January, 1942 my grandfather enlisted in the Australian Army at Geraldton, on the Indian Ocean shore 400 kilometres north of Perth, Western Australia. He was assigned to the 10th Garrison, with the rank of private and service number W47600. Just a fortnight later, on the 16th February, 1942 my grandmother gave birth to her second baby, a little girl she named Wendy Beatrice. She was born at the maternity hospital in Geraldton. On the same day, the reputed fortress of Singapore fell to the Japanese army, 3,500 kilometres to the north. Three days later, on the 19th February, her first-born little girl, my mother, turned four. It was the same day that the bombing of Darwin began 2,500 kms to the north. In just three days, the frontline had moved 1,000 kms closer to home.

On the night of Saturday 21st February, Geraldton was subjected to its first air raid - or so many people thought. Townsfolk were beset with panic and fear as they scrambled for refuge in the sand hills behind the town, contrary to all directions from wardens. My grandmother and her new baby were still in the hospital. The local paper reported that, at the hospital, 'many people had been greatly perturbed and very seriously inconvenienced', and that in future such unannounced 'tests' of the air raid system must be preceded by evacuating patients from the hospital. There was a lot of finger-pointing about who had ordered the test, but some called for lessons to be learnt as the town was obviously unprepared for the war rapidly descending upon it.

The Press reporting makes it very clear that there was widespread panic in the town on the night of the 21st and 22nd of February, from which the hospital was not immune. As my grandmother and her five-day old baby lay in the hospital, the local newspaper was full of reports on building air raid trenches in school grounds, and the evacuation plan for Geraldton - all women, children, the infirm and elderly, carrying only a backpack, a blanket and a water bottle, were to be removed by trains to inland towns, while the Greenough Flats where my grandparents lived were to be totally evacuated and closed to all civilians and occupied by military forces. All radios, telephones and bicycles were to be destroyed.

On the 2nd July, 1942 baby Wendy died, aged just 4½ months. My grandmother always told me that just after Wendy was born, there was a false air raid on Geraldton and all the babies in the hospital, local babies and refugee babies from the East Indies, healthy babies and sick babies, became mixed up in the 'air raid' confusion, after which Wendy was always ill. Her death certificate says she died, in St John of God Hospital in Geraldton, after two days of broncho-pneumonia. She was buried the next day in the Old Greenough Cemetery, among other members of her extended family. The local newspaper reports give us some idea of that awful time of fear, panic and confusion, and confirm my grandmother's memories of the 'air raid' and its consequences.

Chapter 6

Stan Gratte says virtually everyone in Geraldton contacted friends or relatives:

Dad knew someone at Morawa, an inland town about 240kms away. We lived in an empty shop. Mum plastered the shop windows with newspapers. The townspeople were simply great, taking us into their hearts and helping us in all ways possible. We became the 'little evacuees'. We'd seen this term used in English comics, which were still available. We understood the term a bit better then. The adults all expected bombings of coastal towns. I remember meeting the large passenger trains, all fully loaded with people evacuating the north. I talked to one woman who had been bombed. Probably from Broome, where many planes were destroyed and much life lost. My mates Ron and Ian McKillop of Geraldton also turned up, as did others I knew. We went to school and the teacher was a beauty with the cane, as I know. He needed discipline with about eighty kids in the class and he knew how to apply it and retain our respect. My schoolwork improved greatly, due to a few wacks on the hands and some around the legs. I was glad to meet the old teacher many years later and shake his hand.

I took my faithful old pushbike and a quantity of rabbit traps with me. Rabbit skins went up to astronomical prices (to us) as the army wanted the fur to make soldier's felt 'slouch' hats. There were plenty of rabbits around Morawa. Also the townspeople always bought the skinned and gutted rabbits from us for 9 pence each, probably because we were the 'little evacuees.' I still have the fondest of memories for Morawa, particularly Hope Granville, the milkmaid and her horse 'Baldy' for they made us more welcome than anyone, if that were possible.

War news from Britain meant further anxiety for Australians, many who had close ties. They watched as the British authorities, fearing incendiary bombs and poisonous gas, acted fast. The children were Britain's future and they had to be moved away from high density urban centres. Australians wondered what would be the fate of their friends and relatives in Britain and whether they would have to face evacuation too. They read about Britain's 'Evacuate Forthwith,' order, Thursday, 31 August, 1939. In a quasi-military exercise called 'Operation Pied Piper', 1.5 million women and children were evacuated within three days. In the original Pied Piper story, the children never returned, to punish the townspeople for not paying the Pied Piper for rescuing them from a plague of rats. When the young English evacuees did return after scant contact with their birth parents during their formative years, they seemed more like an older sister or brother versions of themselves.

In 1940, after France fell, when coastal towns were perceived as stepping stones for invasion, more people were moved and again in March 1944, when flying bombs threatened London and the Southeast - 3.5 million evacuees in total. *Defence Regulations* informed house occupiers: '...You are required to provide until further notice...accommodation, consisting of shelter and reasonable access to water supply and sanitary conveniences for the persons hereby assigned... Should you fail to carry out this requirement, you will commit an offence.'

Hosts were paid a small sum. As town children met country children, some enjoyed leaving poverty stricken tenements for the good food and bluebell woods of the gentle English countryside, and did not want to return home. They were all bewildered at first, their fathers gone to fight, their mothers left weeping at the station. They found themselves in a strange place, where people spoke with a different accent and could be hostile. Signposts and names of stations had been removed, to confuse invading forces. Some children were welcomed with warmth and understanding and kept in touch with their host family for years after the war. Sadly some children were badly treated, resulting in post war prosecutions. They could not bear to visit their evacuee' home' again, so deep was their trauma.

Australians read British evacuation was 'a dreadful muddle which has 'done wrong' to a very large number of children.' Six months after the first mass evacuation, 43% of unaccompanied children and 86% of those accompanied by mothers, had returned home. Out of 30,000 children evacuated from Sheffield, all but 1,500 had returned by August 1941. This meant large numbers of children remained in or returned to danger areas without education, as teachers could not be in two places at once. In November 1939, there were 80,000 children without schools. Juvenile crime escalated in the ruins, laying the seeds of post war criminal gangs. The film *I Believe in You* with Cecil Parker as a probation officer in Britain's 1950s shows hardened young criminals. Their childhood had been seeing dead bodies, some of whom they had known, before they turned to looting and smashing up houses which had not been bombed. The British Government announced the end of official evacuation on 7 September, 1944. One day later, the first V2 rocket fell on London and a whole new wave of people moved out of the city.

The interwar years had been quiet for most Australian families, mowing lawns in front of their Californian bungalows, housewives spent up to six hours a day preparing food, which arrived at their house by van, cart or bicycle. Only 4.4% of women were employed outside the home in 1933. Walls were cream and green. Tea sets and vases were often Japanese imports. Who would have guessed the country would be in turmoil for fear of an invasion by the ultra-national Japanese Imperial Army.

As part of the war effort, before Japan entered the war, guns were sent off to England. Stan Gratte writes about his father, who was in the rifle club in Geraldton:

> ...the rifle clubs handed in their rifles and these were all sent off to England, a move which was later regretted by the authorities. At the time we were only at war with Germany and Italy.

About 8,000 women and children were evacuated from Malaya and Singapore and about 3, 000 from Hong Kong, mostly to Australia. Appalled at the speed and brutality of the Japanese advance, civilians had to make decisions: were they safe on the home front sending men, money and supplies overseas, accepting refugees, 'doing their bit', or in danger of losing their own country?

By January 1940, Melbourne factories formerly making lipstick cases were now making munitions. In September, the British prison ship *Dunera* docked, filled with Germans, Austrians and Italians fleeing Hitler, some highly educated, but accused of being spies, after an horrific voyage from Britain, after which they arrived pale and emaciated, to be interned at Hay. Newspaper reports of mistreatment by the Pioneer Core running the ship, demonstrated British authorities in so much confusion that the friend was confused with the foe.

Australia with a population of 6,898,541 accepted 15,000 political refugees from Europe. Even before war was declared, children were being moved about the globe in significant numbers, many Jewish children already being rescued. Horace Goldsmith, on *kindertransport* from Germany to England, who was treated very well in England and eventually settled in Australia, was just one small child suddenly parted from everyone he knew:

> Yes, it is now time for me to go away! We are going early in the morning. We go by train on a long journey to Hamburg, where the harbour and the sea is. Papa is taking me. It is a long, long journey in the train and when we get there at night we go to a big hall where there are many children and Papa picks a big boy to look after me for when we get on to the ship tomorrow. That night we sleep together, Papa and I in a hotel and before we go to sleep I say to Papa, 'don't come to the ship to see me off, it will only upset you!' I was nine years old in December 1938. All my family perished, even my grandmother who was so kind and used to make me little cakes.

The typical laconic 'she'll be right' parents had to be frantic to send their young children long distances, especially when they could not communicate with them easily. By 1939, Australia was seventh in the world in telephone ownership, but farms and small towns, where children were usually sent, were without telephones in the 1940s, although some shared party lines. Parents taking or sending children to destinations on long journeys by cars, trucks or trains, returned home and waited impatiently on letters, staring at small, empty beds and praying that their son or daughter was alright.

Meryl Hanford lived at Neutral Bay, in a beautiful house by the water:

> My father, a boat builder was sent to Garden Island to work in the dry dock. People were worried that it would be a Japanese target after Pearl Harbour.

Chapter 6

Peter Grose, author of the ground-breaking book *A Very Rude Awakening* recounts that his father's two unmarried brothers had urged him as a married man with family responsibilities, to stay home:

> In January 1942, he decided that Sydney was too close to the invading Japanese for my mother and five month old me. The three of us travelled by train to my Nan's house in Adelaide, where my mother and I were told to stay put until the war ended. My father enlisted in the army on February 3, 1942 at Collinswood in South Australia, naming my mother as next of kin.

The same concerns were being felt in New Zealand. Jane Putt was a child on a New Zealand farm:

> At the farm in the valley of North Island where I spent my childhood, electricity was put on in 1927 and by the time I was born in 1929, we did have a phone. This was because we just happened to be in the path of the lines from the power station to the towns. Some farmers waited years to be put on. Young boys were trained as runners, to get the message to farmers if there was an invasion.

Sylvia Palmer gives an example of confused thinking about safe locations:

> My husband, who died recently aged 85, told me his three cousins, Karen, June and Thelma Hocking were at Port Kembla, and were sent to my husband's family at Little Hartley, 20 kilometres south-east of Lithgow. My father, sister and brothers all worked at the Small Arms factory - we lived close by it. I don't remember people being worried about being attacked from the air, but we used to play in a hole in a paddock, which we called 'The dungeon', which I realise now was an air raid shelter. We had AA guns on Scenic Hill and at South Bowenfels.

A sequence of turning points like the decisive Battle of Midway changed the appraisal of danger and external threat and children quickly began returning home, only to be sent away again, when the threat returned. The confusion felt at the time is apparent all these years later. Joan Craymer sees things in perspective:

> I understand my friend Lynton Bradford did get in touch and give you a short account of his bike riding experience with the

damage in the Eastern Suburbs. The funny thing was, it had not previously occurred to me that the reason for him going to live at Gerringong with his Aunt Grace was to keep him safe, I had always thought it was because his mother became ill and died about that time, but now it all makes sense.

Bevan Walls only became aware of why he and his mother had 'a holiday' at The Oaks as he read Peter Grose's book *A Very Rude Awakening*, a few years ago.

We lived at Ashfield at the time and I had always known I was three years old when we went to stay at a farmhouse owned by two unpleasant old ladies. There was no one else there other than my mother, and dad came to visit at weekends. At home my dad had put timber screens on all our windows so we could have the lights on and still have air, or maybe they were to reduce the impact of a bomb blast. We had an air raid shelter in the back yard shared with the neighbours, though I don't remember going into it other than when my dad was growing mushrooms after the war. The open spaces at the farm were pleasant and I wandered around outside, playing with pieces of timber off cuts and getting stung by stinging nettles. Mealtimes were not at all pleasant as I remember being locked in their pantry for not eating my dinner, not by mother, but by one of the mean old ladies. I still have a vague memory of the railway station, probably Camden. I don't think we stayed long, a few weeks maybe but I vividly remember my night time fears at Ashfield of imagining someone might walk through the back door at any moment. I can only imagine I heard too much talk of the possibilities of a Japanese invasion. That fear remained with me for many years and into adulthood. There were also the regular reminders of the war: ration cards, dad making his beer, and the regular testing of the local air raid siren at midday. I also remember dad taking me to see the searchlights scanning the night sky near the Heads and the boom gate across the Harbour when we went on the ferry to Manly. I can well imagine we might have even heard the exploding torpedo at our house.

Chapter 6

In any war situation, information is unreliable or non-existent, because of censorship, broken lines of communication and no means of verification. News filtered through and decisions had to be made. To say people were uninformed is an understatement.

Who made the decisions? If it was a woman on her own with children, because her husband was overseas fighting or because she was widowed or single, she had difficulties in making a choice, because she was not used to being allowed to make decisions so large and important. In the Depression, women were criticised for working outside the home. Social mores deemed women ill-equipped for anything other than homemaking and child bearing in the forties. They were subservient, with exciting career opportunities closed except to a few lucky, daring or rich girls. Trying to protect their children when it was not economically viable to relocate meant that women applied for housekeeping jobs, which did not always work out.

Peter Bates:
> I was born in 1936. My mother and I went to a rented house in Armidale and stayed there two or three years. Armidale was pretty small in those days. Initially we went up to a farm where my mother was supposed to be some sort of governess but that didn't work out, so we rented a house. My father, who had been in the first world war joined up in the second. I was an only child. My father visited us once or twice. We were happy there. We got to know people. It was pretty basic. I remember the taps wouldn't run hot for ages.

Women alone also had economic constraints. More than half the population owned or were buying their own house by the end of the forties, the rest were either living with their parents or paying rent. Prices for basic foods in the 1940s were approximately: a four pound loaf of bread, five pence, a quart of milk, seven pence, (sugar was impossible to get), butter one shilling and seven pence a pound, potatoes a shilling a pound, with tea scarce. In the 2nd AIF, before they embarked the rate of pay for a married man with wife and child was up to nine shillings, after they embarked, it was up to eleven shillings. Soldiers had to agree to a dependant's allowance, which was three shillings a day for the first dependant and one shilling a day for each additional dependant. Grounds for cancelling payment to a wife were misconduct: living with another man, giving birth to a child by another man, prostitution, drunkenness and neglect of his children. Compulsory deductions could be made if a soldier was missing or a prisoner of war.

Some women had to have a job, and the war meant there were jobs available. They could not work and care for their children, so for the first time, they looked to relatives and friends for help in child caring. Their relatives in some cases where themselves just scraping a living after the Depression.

Miriam Bates was sent from Lidcombe with her two brothers because the family lived near a possible target:

We went to Penrith, to mum's brother's place for a few months as my parents were worried about the munitions factory near us at Lidcombe. My father was a policeman and had a house attached to the station. We used to go there for holidays and I loved it there. After the Depression, my uncle never had much money and he used to collect wood. I'd ride in the wheelbarrow out to get the wood and have to walk back. He'd put the wood in the back of his 1927 Chevrolet, sell it and use the money to buy food. Mum used to take him up packets and packets of Weet-Bix. I can't say I was frightened about the war, although one of our uncles, a stretcher bearer, was killed. He was only eighteen. When we had a practice air raid warning at school, we had to lie on the floor and cover our heads and I was a bit scared then. Afterwards we moved to Strathfield and my father built a wonderful air raid shelter in the back garden, with interior lighting. We loved it and used to play in there. Then it rained and rained and the shelter flooded. Our toys were ruined!

There was no equal pay for women. In 1941, the ACTU called three conferences to deal with the problem of equal pay, - raising the women's basic rate of pay, which was still only 54% of the male base rate.

In the First World War, women had to struggle with wearing long skirts while driving ambulances, and were disallowed lipstick in case they inflamed the male patient's ardour! That war changed a lot of these perceptions. In WWII, as the men were drafted overseas, the Women's Land Army took over running the farms. One in three workers at munitions, aircraft and shipbuilding works was female by 1943. At this time, the number of women in banking and insurance increased by 31.3 per cent, in rail and air transport by 68.6 per cent. Women in the services had a 'sisterhood' and were rarely alone.

Kev Murphy and his mother fled to Umina, a short train trip from Sydney:
    On the night of the Japanese sub attack on Sydney Harbour, my mum, who had been instructed by my father (at the time encamped in the army in NQ prior to leaving for Egypt) to take me up to my maternal grandmother's house at Umina on the Central Coast, so I might be safe from the expected Japanese landing in Sydney. Some twenty of my cousins had been given similar instructions from my aunts and uncles, but would take some weeks to get their 'flight to safety' effected. For me however, it was instantaneous obedience. My mother was in the Land Army and working sewing gaiters for the soldiers at the Ford motor factory off William Street, and straight away took me in to the city when she got the call in the afternoon. We had to overnight at the People's Palace in Pitt Street as the last train to Woy Woy had gone. We had an upstairs room, with a window on the Harbourside. When the crackling of the guns and the flashing of the searchlights began, it disturbed mum so much she pulled me to the floor and we spent the evening under the single bed. In the morning we walked to Central station and caught the steam train to Woy Woy and out of harm's way. At the time I was three years old and we lived in Stanmore.

Kev provides an insight into the mindset of the Sydneysiders:
    Sydney's population up to the 30s and through the war was heavily in the southern beaches and the eastern suburbs, with the borders of this 'bowl' the Harbour and the Georges and Parramatta Rivers and not too far into the west, protected by the Green Belt; south inhabitation versus north was likely five to one and the northern beaches were just a series of beachside camps visited by homesteaders from Lidcombe and Concord. There were probably

twice as many people in the band stretching from Parramatta to Hornsby as there were on the northern beaches themselves. People in the south zone of Sydney did not go north until the Harbour Bridge was ready for traffic. Even then, growth was stagnant due to the Depression. So it was during the war, panic raged in the southeast. Even the Hills Districts, Bundanoon and Katoomba seemed safe to us in the southern sector of Sydney. It was us southerners who alone had to face the Japs. I well remember the barbed wire stretched along the beaches of Coogee and Maroubra and there were parts where railway sleepers had been embedded in the sand, running into the surf as if they would impede the Toyota and Datsun tanks coming ashore. I'll bet the defence forces didn't lay any impediments onwards from Harbord to Palm Beach although I didn't set foot that way myself until the 50s. Of course, once the war was over, the balance in population quickly righted itself and the northern beaches occasioned the enormous growth we see today. 'Our war' was to be won or lost on the heights of Randwick, we reckoned. With that fuzzy thinking, our parents deemed us safe the moment we exited the reaches of the electric-train network. We were still at risk as far south as Port Kembla but all other points south, west and north (but - careful, don't get too close to Newcastle) were safe as houses.

My permanent return to the southern suburbs didn't happen until 1948, although I often came down in the steam train alone to visit the family in school holiday time from 1944 onwards - a period rich in memories for me as I was soon to see the first of the 'displaced persons' arrive at Circular Quay, the ships' funnels all making the proud announcement with the initials 'DP'.

Some children went backwards and forwards. Bill Geoghlin, who had been in the country:

For some reason we were returned to Sydney but following reports of Japanese lanes overflying Sydney and the midget submarine raid, we went to the bush to the same situation as before, except another sister was in charge of us.

Chapter 6

When Singapore fell February 15, 1942, there was a lot of anti-British feeling in Australia. In her book *When the Children Came Home,* Julie Summers describes how young Robert Arbuthnott arrived after the fall of Singapore with his family and was beaten up by four 17 year old Australian students at Knox Grammar School. They broke his nose.

It was a sobering thought that while inland country towns in Australia were less likely to be threatened by enemy action, in a time of emergency there could be many things country people could be called upon to do as part of the national war effort. In the event of a coastal attack or bombing raids on the cities the people in country districts would have to play an important part in the plans for the evacuation of women and children. Invasion fears are reflected in boxed advertisements in the Press, showing the energetic movement of evacuees. Country people offered help such as, 'Evacuee's children's nurse has vacancies for children in country home', and coastal people looked for refuge with advertisements like, 'Soldier's wife, two children, wants country board', for instance.

Chapter 7
Will We Lose Our Country?

Whenever there was a raid ...they were all turned out of the factory to the trenches because it was assumed that an aircraft factory would be a priority target. Everyone was sure the Japs would be back.

– Cassie Thornley

Chapter 7

When war was declared, there was a mix of emotions fear, excitement, patriotic fervour. Those touched by it before were full of dread. Stan Gratte still remembers his mother's face even after all this time:

I came home in the afternoon to find my mother in a most unusual mood. She had a look of intense sadness, of which I still have a picture in my mind. She said, 'War has been declared. We are at war.' Mum had three brothers in WWI, all gassed or shot or both. Her boyfriend had been killed at the Somme in France and she well knew what was to come about.

There is no doubt that the level of fear and concern was great in the civilian population and they reacted by protecting their children. Some were sent more than a day's travel away:

Before the war, Australian politicians of all persuasions first followed the policy of appeasement, (notably Robert Menzies). When war was declared by Britain, Australian eyes met, knowing that from that moment, their lives would change from the ordinary to the extraordinary. Australians would follow Britain into war without question. Britain was a major trading partner, British banking dominated the Australian scene, British immigrants were still pouring into the country, and British history was taught in schools. Australia looked to the British Navy to protect her shores and when Australians left their native shores; their first destination was inevitably Britain. It first appeared that Australia's role in the war would be as a main supplier of meat, wool and dairy goods. US President Roosevelt would say later, 'food is a weapon of total war fully as important as guns, planes and tanks'.

By 1940, Australians were reading about the London Blitz. On Saturday, 7 September, 375 German bombers throbbed their way across Kent to London - too many for the RAF fighters to stop. They struck at the docks, industrial and trade heartland of London. Incendiaries and high explosives rained down into the sheets of flame already consuming warehouses, factories and homes. Cecil Beaton's photograph of three year old Eileen Dunne sitting up in a hospital bed with a bandaged head, clutching a battered teddy bear, started his career. Jack Buchanan sang *Everything Stops for Tea*. The British scanned long lists of casualties and dead in the newspapers.

A Carefree War

In Australia, about 7,000 residents, mostly male, including more than 1,500 British nationals, deemed 'enemy aliens' were interned. A further 8,000 people were interned after being detained overseas by allies. More than 12,000 people were herded into camps, even if domiciled in Australia for years. People hastily requested naturalisation.

With so much complacency, why were Australian civilians so ready to believe a Japanese invasion was imminent after the fall of Singapore? How did the military perceive the situation? Were the governments prepared?

Invasion fears are deep seated in the island that is Australia. Suspicion had fallen onto different groups in the past - French, Russians, Chinese and for quite a while, the Japanese. The French explored Botany Bay and settled Akaroa in New Zealand and invited settlers there. Until Napoleon was defeated by Nelson at the Battle of Trafalgar, 1805, they were a definite presence in this region. The Russians were occasionally viewed with deep distrust. In 1882, when three friendly Russian navy ships – the *Africa*, *Vestnik*, and *Plastun* docked in Melbourne, the Press sparked widespread fears of a Russian invasion, but after things were sorted out, a civic ball was given in their honour! The Chinese were also seen as potential invaders, despite the fact that they had explored the coast in Confucius' time and returned to their own country. Japan has been the only country that has actually attacked Australian soil, making invasion fears a reality.

Distrust of Japan was publicly demonstrated as far back as 1896, when reports of Japanese trading interests led to a Premier's Conference. The trading proposal by the Japanese was refuted by Australia (and later by New Zealand). The Conference recommended that all Australian colonies extend their legislation to exclude coloured persons. Japanese and Chinese labourers were deemed 'undesirable' in the following 1901 *Immigration Restriction Act*, which was the basis of the *White Australia Policy*, decisively carried by the Australian Labor Party, at the time of the 1901 Federation. The *Policy* also addressed threats of hostile invasion and defence against invaders. As a shaping of national identity and with the appearance of protecting the Australian wage earner, the *WAP* brought with it a fixation on whiteness. The intent of the *Policy* ignored the fact that global labour and expertise had been brought in to accomplish world class projects in Australia. For instance, in the building of the Hawkesbury River Bridge from 1886-89, 3,000 workers, most from overseas, descended on the river banks with their expertise to build the bridge for its American managers. A local pub was called the 'All Nations Hotel'.

Australians were reinforced in their invasion concerns with slogans like 'yellow peril' and 'populate or perish'. Widely read invasion novels, cartoons and comics said that only as a nation with a clear identity and racial purity could Australia react powerfully to an invasion attempt. So the majority thinking was that Australia should prepare for invasion, the exclusion of Chinese and Japanese workers was an imperative, and the 'right kind' of immigrant was needed to build up and defend the Australian way of life. Enthusiastic in the belief that accelerated British migration would make Sydney the first Australian city to reach a population of one million, Sir Arthur Rickard founded the Millions Club in 1912, but the millions would have to be white Anglo Saxon child migrants, of above average intelligence and perfect physical wellbeing from the UK. This screening resulted in British brother and sister potential migrants being parted because one of them wore glasses or one had not had measles.

In the terms of the day the *White Australia Policy* expressed the fear of Australia being isolated and ringed by hostile Asian countries. Current sentiment was clear when for the first time in 160 years of European settlement, Australia *was* directly threatened, Prime Minister John Curtin said: '...this country shall remain forever the home of the descendants of those people who came here in peace in order to establish in the South Seas an outpost of the British race'. Deep seated racism later led The Advisory War Council to decide on 12 January, 1942, that' no black American troops would be accepted in Australia since it could affect ...the maintenance of the *White Australia Policy* in post-war settlement'. This slur on our ally was hastily erased.

Within hours of Japan entering the war, Japanese men working in the Torres Strait and West Australian pearling industry were arrested, because they were familiar with the coastline and reefs of Torres Strait. Australians had purchased copies of their charts in 1923, used by the

Allies. Over a million copies of a Japanese book *The Inevitable Anglo-Japanese War* published in 1935 had been sold. Wartime advertisements for Liberty Loans emphasised the destruction of Australian country towns, with vivid black and white drawings. In 1937, the *Sunday Times* reported a party from an Australian farm were guests at Vancouver's Canadian Pacific Exhibition and a Mr Gradbury of Goulburn told interviewers that. '... the Empire's greatest danger is a Japanese invasion of Australia'. There is a mountain of evidence about spying on both sides, of course. Les Reedman recalls that the bags of a Japanese diplomatic mission were searched in 1938:

> They were found to have maps in their bags with pencil marks on strategic points from Port Stephen to Shoalhaven.

A letter sent to Prime Minister John Curtin by Mr Herbert Yeates, Member of the Legislative Assembly for East Toowoomba, Queensland stated that '...a Mr Griffiths, a highly respected citizen, had met an officer in the Japanese Naval Reserve in Singapore six years previously who had spoken of plans to invade Australia if Singapore fell.'

To aggravate invasion fears, there were soon sporadic instances of bombing and shelling around Australia.

Australians kept their spirits up in different ways, some by keeping busy, some by prayer, some with 'blackout parties' where special 'bomb cocktails' were served - 'high explosive' and 'delayed action', to name but a few. At some parties, masks were worn, those without masks being fined, proceeds going to the RAAF Comforts Fund.

While many civilians became increasingly uneasy, rumours and panic swept Canberra in the autumn of 1942, according to historian Paul Hasluck, and intelligence advisors, like civilians, made tentative predictions, trying to piece together bits of information to learn Japanese intentions. General MacArthur told the War Council he did not think Japan would invade. Allied intelligence was amazingly efficient, in decoding difficult German and Japanese messages, working together with Bletchley Park, but the Japanese themselves were arguing about invasion proposals and did not have a cohesive policy.

Eddie Ward, Labor opposition politician, was supposedly leaked evidence by a Major working in the Secretary for Defence Office, about the Menzies' government's 'defeatist' and 'treacherous' plan that large tracts of Australia's north would be abandoned to the invaders - The Brisbane Line. He spoke about it publicly at Preston, Victoria. A similar concept had already been rejected by Prime Minister Curtin and the Australian War Cabinet and they refuted Ward's comments, but Ward continued his accusations during late 1942 and early 1943. The idea that it was an actual defence strategy, gained momentum after General Douglas MacArthur referred to it during a Press conference in March 1943, as the 'Brisbane Line'. Ward claimed that some relevant files had been removed but a resulting Royal Commission concluded that no such documents had existed.

MacArthur, in his own memoir *Reminiscences*, stated that if an invasion did occur the Australian military would establish a line of defence following the Darling River from Brisbane to Adelaide. But in those nervous days, civilians quickly had the idea of the Brisbane Line firmly fixed in their minds.

The idea lives on. In his book *The Brisbane Line*, Hugh MacMaster says: 'According to many historians, the Brisbane Line was studied as a sensible fall back in which a badly depleted Australian army, whose major forces were still abroad, would trade space for time to build up its strength engage allies and bring divisions back to Australia. It was a sensible sort of strategic concept - as the Russians were to demonstrate in their 'scorched earth policy', of leaving an advancing enemy nothing of worth. And it was a concept feared by the most senior Japanese general to study a possible invasion of Australia, Lieutenant- General Yamashita, nicknamed the 'Tiger of Malaya' for his defeat of the British, Australian and Indian forces in Malaya and Singapore.

An Army Development Guide drew a 'Newcastle Line, north of Newcastle and arcing around Port Augusta, the area contained by it estimated as a heartland without which Australia cannot survive in its present state. Currently we are dependent on our allies in a national crisis, and this of course was the situation in 1942.

Being convinced of an invasion did not give anybody certainty of when, where and how it would happen. Australia seethed with ideas and rumours. *The Times* in London mused that Japan might attempt to establish naval and aerial bases at Darwin, and perhaps Broome and Wyndham and launch attack on coastal cities from there. Residents around Australia were convinced the Japanese were going to land where *they* were. There are numerous accounts of Japanese landings, mostly unsubstantiated. One story is that the enemy set up a radio on Middle Brother Mountain, near Taree, and a small number of Japanese were captured at Old Bar. An imminent landing at Coffs Harbour was feared. Plans were in place to move residents, stock and produce to the Tablelands, which had a fortress mentality. Barriers were built near Ebor, half way between Armidale and Coffs Harbour in May 1942, with road ends packed with 1,800 pounds of gelignite. To prevent the roadway being bypassed, the expensive Ebor Tank Barrier was constructed, the longest of all barriers built in WWII.

With concerns that Tasmania would be invaded, largely because of the state's zinc industry, children were evacuated from Hobart. Geraldton, West Australia was also prepared for the worst. Civilians, apprehensive after the disappearance of HMAS *Sydney* off the Geraldton coast in November 1941, were aware of German subs in striking distance of the west coast. Air raid shelters were dug for the 600 school children in the isolated city. Were they going to be part of a scorched earth policy?

Missions at Roper River and the surrounding country were emptied because that was imagined another possible entry for the Japanese. At Yeppoon, locals thought there would be a pincer movement from them to Hervey Bay. An eccentric local lady at Yeppoon said a Japanese submarine had landed and she saw Japanese coming ashore for fresh water. She was 'put away'... but who knows?

By late 1941, civilians were convinced of an invasion of Sydney. A People's Army was formed. Members of the co-ordinating committee included Lieutenant-Colonel Hyman, the President of the Retired Servicemen's League, Charlie Nelson, the General President of the Miner's Association and Jim Healey, the General Secretary of the Waterside Workers' Federation. Women's voluntary groups were drawn on for this army. In the Ku-ring-gai section on the North Shore of New South Wales alone there were 300 women members.

Chapter 7

All the talk was of war, but there was still an underlying air of unreality. On 31 May, 1942, a group of AWAS coming back off leave to 2nd Australia Corps at Burnside Homes, Parramatta, were on the Manly ferry followed by the Japanese midget submarines. By the time they had taken the train from Wynyard to Parramatta, and the bus to camp, there were a series of alerts, blackouts and continual gunfire. The AWAS, wearing tin hats and gas masks crouched under the tables, cursing the Generals for putting them through this exercise - not realising it was the real thing! It was not until the following day that the Harbour raid was common knowledge, and then it was relegated to page 3. In May 1942, there was an increase in Japanese submarine movement along the eastern coast of Australia. In 1942, NF461970 Steward, Jenny, (later Johns), was peering through a narrow slit watching shipping in Port Kembla, working two hours on and two hours off and scanning the Harbour for intruders:

Everyone was aware of the daring raid and knew it could be repeated.

Cassie Thornley remembers her cousin Beryl worked in an Aircraft Factory, one of the 600 or so from all over the country converted to build Australia's only homemade aircraft, the Beaufort Bomber:

It was based on the English one, but the Brits refused to send us the plans because they were a war secret, so ours had many parts, including the landing gear, redesigned. Beryl's factory had previously made motorcar parts. It was at Marrickville. There were trenches out the back, everyone tried to get all the children away from that area. Whenever there was a raid (or perhaps ships sighted off the coast?) they were all hurried out of the factory to the trenches, because it was assumed an aircraft factory would be a priority target. Everyone was sure the Japs would be back.

The choice of children being victims of a ruthless invading army or fleeing to a quiet farm out of harm's way was not a simple one. Some children left the safe haven of their home, and returned only to be sent away again, in the uncertainty of the times.

While the public protested and bureaucrats procrastinated; families evacuated their children and women joined groups organising themselves against air raids. The Air Raid Post in Victoria enrolled over 1,000 women in the metropolitan area, learning first aid work, stretcher bearing, clerical and mobile unit work and training as aircraft spotters and telephonists.

If there was lingering doubt about Japanese policies for domination, on 4 April, 1942, Australian newspapers were full of seizures of Japanese arms in the State of Sao Paulo, in south Central Brazil, described as a 'hotbed of fifth columnists.' The first Japanese immigrants had arrived in Brazil in 1908, to work on the coffee plantations, the largest concentration being in São Paulo and Paraná. The plan was to take over the immediate area as a stronghold. Eighty Germans, Italians, and Japanese were arrested. Naval officers were found in possession of uniforms, photographs of ships, and strategic Brazilian maps. At Sao Paulo, Brazil, police arrested a Japanese army captain who had masqueraded as a woman cook for five years in the household of a director of an important Brazilian war-materials concern! Another one was posing as a dentist! Arms were smuggled into shops and hidden. No similar cell was discovered in Australia, although 'information gathering spying' had gone on for years. Perhaps this is another indication that the Japanese did not intend to invade Australia - not in the 1940s at least.

Eventually the tide of war changed and evacuees returned, but the heartache and fear always remained. Shirley Killeen remarked that we should remember those who were left:

I went to the birthday party of my friend, who is eighty, recently. Another friend said, 'How marvellous that you have been friends all these years.' The eighty-year-old said, 'No, she went away and left me.' She meant when I was evacuated for two years and she wasn't.

Chapter 8
Keep Calm and Carry On

Mum wouldn't go into it, (the air raid shelter), because
she said there were spiders. So we put a mattress over
the dining room table and sat underneath.

– Bev Kingston

A Carefree War

In December 1941, NSW country trains pulling out of the city were packed. By February 1942, the newspapers stated the NSW government had assisted 2,000 civilians to evacuate from the city into the country, but many stayed put and some drove into danger deliberately to be with loved ones.

In London, Queen Elizabeth, (later the Queen Mother), famously said, 'The children can't go without me. I can't leave the King, and of course the King won't go, earning her the undying affection of Londoners in the Blitz, when many crowned heads of Europe were leaving their countries. Churchill was also a familiar figure in the ruins, cigar clenched between his teeth, offering a cheery word to shop keepers, who put up notices saying, 'Business as Usual' in the ruins of their premises. *Manchester Guardian* on 19 August, 1940:

480 British Children sent to Private Homes in Australia

Last night there was a touch of near-weeping about a few children. But at the dock today they marched stoutly, in tartan, blazer, brown shirt, shorts, infants' skirts and schoolgirls' skirts, halting, breaking ranks to watch a porter wheeling a woolly toy lamb on wheels. Gas masks went on board only to come ashore later. Then it was time for us to be off. The last sight was 'thumbs up' at the portholes'.

British children were evacuated to Victoria between 1940 and 1945, following an agreement between the British and Australian governments and boarded out with families. The Children's Welfare Department oversaw the allocation of the children to their custodians and their welfare. Sixty- two children and young people came to Western Australia under the Overseas Children Scheme.

In Australia, people stayed put for various reasons: mothers of large families in poorer suburbs were too busy rearing children to worry about something that might never happen, seeing evacuation for those with money and said they would sit tight until the government told them to move. A Mrs Witcher, with eleven children, the youngest aged eighteen months, stayed at home. 'Besides, Dad says they'll never take Singapore.' she said.

Chapter 8

Jack Davey sang *Our Air Raid Shelter* on the radio in 1942:

There's no more room now in our air raid shelter,
There's Aunt 'n Gran 'n Dad 'n Mum 'n me.
And when the sirens sound we all run helter-skelter,
Just Aunt 'n Gran 'n Dad 'n Mum 'n me.

In air raids, civilians were told to walk, not run into shelters, (the enemy didn't like you keeping cool!), and to: 'Keep in readiness by your bedside a torch, a candle with matches, some money, a warm sweater, and a pair of slacks. In the case, have a roll of bandages, cotton wool, drinking water, sticking plaster, a bottle of iodine, some cakes of plain chocolate, a pair of low-heeled shoes and a change of clothes. They were advised to keep their bath full of water, turn off the gas and electricity and cover food in case of flying glass splinters.

When Bev Kingston and her family went to North Queensland in 1946, she found a level of disapproval of those who had evacuated. We sat it out back in Manly, me and Mum under the dining room table, Dad braving the submarine barrage across the Harbour to go to work every day on the ferry. My parents were probably too poor to send me away but I was also only a toddler – we lived in Manly just a few doors up from the barbed wire entanglements on the beach. Dad constructed an air raid shelter in the backyard according to the plans given in the *Women's Weekly* I believe, but Mum wouldn't go into it because she said there were spiders. So when Manly was shelled from the sea we put a mattress over the dining room table and sat underneath. The people next door had their windows broken by the shells.

A census taken by the local air raid wardens of those desiring to evacuate resulted in 200 residents moving to the Tablelands.

Shelters in the backyards were usually a deep trench covered by a corrugated water tank cut in half and covered in sandbags with steps down inside. People left their comfortable living rooms, grabbing warm blankets, pulled wellingtons on and went down the shelter steps, where muddy rainwater collected. Spiders and the occasional frog shared the space with stores of food, first aid items, essential tools, torches and water. Some people took personal documents and photo albums, a favourite party dress or special pair of shoes, along with the pet dog, rabbit or cat.

Geoff Hoad remembers discussions about leaving, but nothing happened:
> My family talked about two main things in the war, my uncle being on the ferry that the subs followed into the Harbour, and my mum being told to go up to Junee because she was expecting me - she stayed with my dad!

John Squires says his wife's parents changed their minds:
> My wife, who was a year younger than me, with her older sister, my age, prepared for evacuation from Paddington to Gunning, with some other local friends, but cooler minds prevailed and her parents couldn't part with them, so their little Shirley Temple's farm overalls remained unused. Her father built a slit trench in their tiny backyard, beneath a three storey building that would have buried them had a bomb or shell struck.

Charmaine Piaud thinks they had every reason to go, but for some explained reason they did not:
> I remember the attack on Sydney Harbour as we were down in our air raid shelter and a next door neighbour had a heart attack there. She died several weeks later on my second birthday. I was supposed to go to the Blue Mountains, my mother to accompany me but to no known relatives. My father and my brother who was born in 1929 were to stay behind. I don't know why the move was cancelled. Mum never said.

Barry Hishion lived by one airfield and his only relatives lived next to another one, so they stayed put:
> At Port Kembla, barbed wire entanglement had been laid along Port Kembla beach because enemy submarines were active along the coast. On the night of November 4, 1942 a Lockheed Hudson that had been searching for enemy submarines during bad weather, crashed into the escarpment west of Dapto killing the crew of four.

Chapter 8

It was bad weather, not submarine activity that saw the US tanker Cities Service Boston wrecked off Bass Point at Shellharbour on May 21, 1943. Four soldiers from the 6th Machine Gun Battalion (AIF) patrolling the coast that day, lost their lives whilst helping to save the 62 man crew. The steelworks remained safe throughout the war with production running 24 hours.

My parents had great concern for the safety of their children and with good reason. Our home in Birdwood Rd 'Bass Hills', later designated Georges Hall, overlooked Bankstown Aerodrome from high on a ridge above. Built in 1940, the 640 acres of bushland had been reclaimed then levelled to form a primitive airfield. Primarily it became a training base for pilots, using two seater Tiger Moths to do circuits and bumps before the unit was transferred to Point Cook in Victoria. This happened following Pearl Harbour and after the Federal Government had acquired military equipment from America through the Lend Lease scheme. Huts were built, along with hangars for Bell Airacobra P39 fighter planes that arrived later with American pilots. These were the first of many military aircraft to be based at Bankstown, seeing it become a prime target for any invading force.

When Japanese midget submarines entered Sydney Harbour on 31 May, 1942, one torpedoed and sank HMAS *Kuttabul*. That night the aerodrome erupted with noise so great, that all thought an invasion had come. Searchlights combed the sky and with confused radio reports, it took a long time before events on the Harbour came to be known. In the frantic action for pilots to answer the call, one plane did not take sufficient time to warm up and crashed across the Georges River at Chipping Norton. De Havilland Aircraft built a very large hangar and set up production of the Mosquito bomber, providing employment for many people. It was there that I later served my apprenticeship as a sheet metal worker during production of the Vampire jet fighter.

Could we children have been sent to the country for safety? Our only country relatives were at Richmond, where another air base was located, a prime target, so we stayed at home. We gained a sense of security when soldiers became camped on the vacant land sloping down to the main gate of the aerodrome. Their stay was short and we believe that they went on to number among the heroes of Kokoda. Each night three searchlights combed the skies and picked up any planes in flight. One effective unit was located on nearby Black Charlie's Hill overlooking the aerodrome, offering a false sense of security. In a large bunker under a hill that over looked Bankstown, there was located the operations centre for the war in the South Pacific. It was heavily guarded by soldiers and very secret. It was only after the war that its operations were revealed. Along with mates I crawled through a hole to view and discover the abandoned site in 1946. We weren't the only ones to do so. In 1945 and prior to the war's end, the Fleet Air Arm of the Royal Navy took over the aerodrome, naming it HMS *Nabberley*.

Some mothers took their children away but were so unhappy they went back home. Ida, who signed her letters 'your loving wife', left her husband Frank in Tully, taking daughters Mary and Jane with her to rooms in Stanthorpe, where she knew nobody. In March 1942, she wrote to Frank, to say her mother had decided not to come with them as she thought it would be too cold. Ida sent a wire to him to say she might come home next week, '... you'll probably think we are all mad, and perhaps we are ... accommodation is very scarce (and) ... you don't know how it feels to walk into a strange, cheerless looking double room and think that is home.' She says her landlady; Mrs Finn is a good, kind, hard working little woman. 'Most of the places you go to look at are full of 'Don'ts', and start off laying down the law about what you can do and what you can't do. The old lady is still here. I think we will even get used to her cough.' Ida ends the letter with, 'Oh, well, dear, I will just wait and see what you say about us going home. I hope we will be able to. All my love and lots from Jane and Mary'.

Other wives and mothers followed their husbands, sometimes with children, into danger zones, to be near their loved ones. Georgia Newton was born in 1942. Her mother moved constantly to be near her husband, who was in the Navy on HMAS *Canberra*. On 9 August,

Chapter 8

1942, in the Battle of Savo Island, off the Solomon's, seven Japanese battle cruisers struck the lead ship *Canberra* in a surprise attack and it was finally destroyed by American torpedoes:

My brother was seven years old and my mother was pregnant with me when my father, who was in the Navy, was killed on board HMAS *Canberra*. I was born one month later. My mother moved to Sydney when he was based there, and then took the steam train to Brisbane and moved there. She must have thought it was better to be near him and in danger than left at home to worry. Many wives did that when their husbands were in the services.

Some people were disapproving of evacuees, saying they should stay and help with the war effort. The *Sydney Morning Herald*, Thursday, 6 January, 1942: Ruth Watt replied to a letter writer criticising her and her friends for removing their children, as 'a flagrant example of utter selfishness on behalf of a favoured few.' She said, Being one of the four mothers who have taken a house between them I would like to state ... mothers are naturally anxious to have their children in comparative safety ... it is obvious to the meanest intelligence that the aforesaid parents, instead of being criticised for sending their children to the country should be commended for organising a household where children can lead a normal life and at the same time allow their parents to carry on with their war work.

If you were desperate parents without relatives, friends were the next option, even if they were afar and without a telephone. Heather Baker's parents turned to people they knew from their Scottish village:

In 1941 I was eight and my brother was four. We lived at Mosman and were quite close to where the Japanese submarines came in. My father was away fighting in the Middle East, (he was at Tobruk), and my mother worked at the Menzies Hotel. Some friends of the family, the Houstons, lived at Tenterfield. Mrs Houston had worked in the same wool mill in Scotland as our grandmother. Mr Houston was a retired baker. We stayed with them when we first came to Australia, in Neutral Bay. One day, my mother came home to us two children and the Scottish lady supposed to be looking after us was under the table with a mattress on the top.

A Carefree War

We were in our beds. She decided to send us to the Houstons. We went on a long, long rail trip as we had to pull into sidings and let troop trains go by. Mrs Houston did not have any children and I don't think she was overjoyed to have us, but we stayed two years, attending Tenterfield School. I think all the other children were locals. My father visited us once, going AWOL, and unbeknownst to him, my brother had mumps and he caught them. My mother visited us when she could. The Houstons did not have a telephone. I suppose they wrote to each other.

Andrew Kyle with his brothers - 'Rabbit Boys' in Oberon.

HMAS Kuttabul *was torpedoed and sunk by Japanese submarines with 21 Navy personnel aboard - Sydney Harbour, 31 May, 1942*

Anthony Healey in his dad's tin helmet, 1942

Valda McDonald with her Uncle Maurice Jeffriess at Werris Creek in 1941

P + D. Harley.
Form 1a

Circular Ev. 42.
STATE EMERGENCY SERVICES (VICTORIA) EVACUATION COMMITTEE.

EVACUATION OF CHILDREN.

ADVICE REGARDING CLOTHING, LUGGAGE, AND FOOD.

To Parents.

The following notes are printed for your information and help in equipping your children for the journey if their evacuation becomes necessary.

CLOTHING.

(A) For School Children.

Children should be warmly clad for the journey as wearing clothes is the easiest way of carrying them.

The amount of clothing children can take with them on the evacuation journey is limited to what can be conveniently carried and to the room available for luggage in the train.

After you receive advice as to where your children have been billeted in the Reception Area, it will be necessary for you to send them further clothing by rail.

Besides the clothes (including overcoats) which your children should

State Emergency Services in Victoria advise what to pack for evacuation

DANGER-ZONE. This street is in heart of large Sydney suburb. One of the brick terrace houses is occupied by Mr. and Mrs. L. Devaecke, who have three young daughters. Their safety is first consideration of parents.

EVACUATION ADVICE. Mrs. Devaecke, with the guidance of Miss Una Parr, fills in details for Government Evacuation form. Blonde daughters Shirley (14), Norma (5), and Beryl (12), eagerly watch the process.

SKILLED PACKING ability comes in handy when three daughters' requirements have to be crammed into minimum space. Mother supervises while Beryl (left) folds pyjamas.

City Evacuees Trek to A New World

PLANNING the evacuation of Sydney's children immediately on the realisation of the Pacific war, has given N.E.S. authorities many headaches. Voluntary evacuations, which started the day after the Japs bombed Pearl Harbor, have continued in an ever-increasing stream. Rush for forms for participation in the Government scheme showed the city's readiness to protect its younger generation — 200,000 of whom are of school age. This series by "Sunday Sun" color photographer, N. Herfort, typifies countless similar scenes of departures for new worlds in the country.

GOODBYE! Shirley, Beryl and Norma wave to their parents from train window as they start off for new home. Hostesses undertake to give evacuated children special care

HEALTHY COUNTRY LIFE won't do the Devaecke sisters any harm. Accommodation for evacuated children is being arranged in private homes, boarding-houses, hotels in safe centres.

ONE OF THE THRILLS. Two small evacuees from Double Bay learn to ride on a farm 40 miles from the city. Fabian helps his aunt, Mrs. Cooney, to hold the horse while brother John swings into the saddle for first time.

Sunday Sun Colour Feature, February 8, 1942

Cassie and Jim Thornley in a hand tinted photograph

Bruce Baskerville's grandparents with their oldest daughter, Geraldton, WA

Horace Goldsmith, part of
kindertransport *from Germany to*
Britain, who later settled in Australia

Bevan Walls and playmate Mick
from next door outside their Ashfield
air raid shelter

Kevin Murphy races past Lion Island as his neighbour
Mrs Booth (left) chats on Ocean Beach sands

Kevin's mum Noeline balances her charge
on the knee with her mother Maud
(Marsie) and sister Muriel looking on

Kevin Murphy on his trike in 1942

*Maud (Marsie) Lamont, sunning
on the verandah*

*Maud and her youngest child, Noeline,
1942*

*Etna Street: The Gosford home of real estate agent and Gosford councillor
Donald Lamont - Kevin's uncle, circa 1945*

Bev Kingston outside her Manly home air raid shelter, 1942

Cotswold, Armidale, a beautiful old home opened as a nursery, kindergarten and prep school in 1942 by a Miss M Buik

Heather Baker, aged 8 and her brother aged 4 being visited by their mother, at the Houstons, Tenterfield

Marie and John Costello with mother Eileen, travelled from Wollongong to Glen Innes, a 12 hour train trip

Heather Baker and her mum visiting Mrs Houston again

Jacqueline Parker aged 10, (right, front row) at boarding school, Bathurst 1944.

Jacqueline Parker (r) with friends Gwen and Francis at Bathurst

Shore School boys, Mt Victoria

*Shore School Prep. boarders, Third and Fourth Form outside
the Guest Hotel at Mount Victoria, 1942*

Bob Taylor's aunt's refreshment stall at the railway station

Bob Taylor's cousins and their mother after they had cleaned out Gran's fowl yard

Bruce H Crawford aged 18 months

Joyce Taylor ready for school

Eric Pfeiffer (driving) and Max Craymer in the front seat with children

Evacuee children at Tahmoor Holiday Home.

McCattie Park Bathurst, Betty and Lola Wooley

Lola, Betty and Lesley (kneeling) Wooley at Monument to Blaxland and Wentworth

Chapter 9
Empty Desks

My sister never forgave my mother for sending her away ...
She reckoned mum just wanted to go to work and have us looked after.
My sister was 14 at the time and only spent one year there.

— Jacqueline Parker

A Carefree War

A nn Carolan:

Japan bombed Pearl Harbour and Australia came into the War 7 December, 1941. School holidays came soon afterwards, while the Japanese moved rapidly south. By the time school resumed (early February, 1942), many Sydney boarding schools had decided to move their children away from potential danger. My school was St. Vincent's College at Potts Point. The boarders spent 1942 at a guest house in Katoomba. The rest of the children (me included) remained at Potts Point.

The boarding house they used was 'Wagunyah'. Most city boarding schools did the same, so you would be talking of thousands of school children. Lots of families chose to move away from harbourside suburbs, like Vaucluse, (which was not a 'posh' area then). I can think of quite a few people who did so, particularly in Potts Point. We all felt safer as the Americans began to arrive during 1942. The whole area was khaki. England wasn't going to protect us from a Japanese invasion.

For the next four years that whole area was full of American servicemen - thankfully. The submarine attack was just down the street. My parents didn't tell me to stay home from school. I travelled from Kogarah to Potts Point as usual, and nothing was spoken of that day about the noise and shelling of the previous night.

My old school friends and I often remark on the change in the times. Children nowadays are sheltered so much. They can't even cross a street. Cars are told to dodge them instead of the reverse!

I know that the Rose Bay Convent girls moved to Bundanoon, but I have no memory of where all the other boarding schools went.

Someone should really write about those days in Sydney - all the little things. How many people now realise Sydney was in danger of small landings from the huge number of enemy subs off the coast. They were sinking the ships going up to New Guinea. At school we watched the troop ships leaving Woolloomooloo. There was the 'brown out', food and petrol rationing, and my grandfather's little fishing boat at Burraneer Bay was 'requisitioned' by the Government. Imagine Sydney with no little boats! Anyway, no-one complained with all the young men away fighting, being killed or taken prisoner.

Pupils were evacuated from schools all over Australia, to ensure their safety, to reassure anxious parents and to vacate buildings for the military and hospitals for civilian casualties. Even after the Battle of the Coral Sea and the Battle of Midway, the Australian government continued to warn an invasion was possible until mid-1943. Schools had to make disruptive and expensive decisions in an area of uncertainty. How long would war in the Pacific last? Would there be war on Australian soil?

Dr Wade was Headmistress at MLC from 1941-1959. Part of her reminiscences read:

> The war, of course, brought with it constant anxiety. The school's administrators had to be prepared for the possible need for evacuation to the country and to contend with the ever-present danger of bombing and even the threat of invasion. Life during the first two years of the decade at least was lived very much in a state of constant alert. While many of the girls, not appreciating the full gravity of the situation, may well have enjoyed the drama and excitement of air raid alerts and trench drill, those responsible for the well-being of the school and its students must have found the experience exhausting and harrowing.

As the Japanese advance gained momentum and as attack from the air and even invasion became more likely, extraordinary measures had to be taken for pupils' protection and contingency plans made. Apart from the physical dangers there was anxiety that the school's buildings would be taken over for military use or that evacuation to the country would be necessary. The attitude of parents was another source of worry and the fluctuating enrolments reflected parental fears for the safety of their daughters'.

A Carefree War

The MLC School Council decided to remain in Burwood but: 'In the meantime protective measures had been taken. The halls of the Tower Wing had been converted into air raid shelters, and bags and sand to fill them had been purchased as a protection against incendiary bombs. Sandbags and buckets of sand littered almost every corridor and doorway. By March 1942 air raid trenches had appeared in the field - they were provided by the Burwood Municipal Council - and just over a month later these had been boarded, floored and provided with draining. MLC was prepared for the worst. Air raid drill became a regular feature of school life and the pupils quickly became accustomed to the routine. Six long peals of the school bell and the whole school would spring into action:

> The air raid bell rings. We very quickly form a double line in our classroom and wait for our form mistress. As soon as we are allowed to go, we hurry to our shelter - a table in the boarders' dining room. Chairs are quickly pulled out and we crawl under. We put on our ear pads, a handkerchief or rubber in our mouth, and sit there till the bell rings again telling us we may return to our classroom.

Some schools in danger zones evacuated their boarders, whilst the day pupils remained but had staggered hours of school attendance as a safety measure. Some schools rented properties, to relocate pupils but some had to buy new premises, which had to be altered. Some bought large old houses and retained them after the war: Scots College, for instance, moved to Bathurst and kept the residence.

Another difficulty was a wartime shortage of teachers. By 1943, over 100 small schools in NSW were closed for lack of teachers. The assistant general secretary of the Teachers' Federation, Mr Kennett said that at the outbreak of war, the teaching service was under- staffed according to accepted educational standards, and now it was 1,000 short of the 1939 figures. There were about 900 vacancies in schools which were at present staffed, and in some cases teachers had classes of more than 50 or 60 pupils. The *British Education Act*, (which was followed at that time in Australia), recommended a maximum of 30 pupils in secondary classes. The NSW Federation requested the release of 50 per cent of the teachers in the Forces, to relieve the alarming shortage in schools. It also asked for the repeal of the *Married Women (Lecturers and Teachers) Act,* which automatically dismissed women teachers on their marriage, so that women will be able to continue in permanent service. Over 1,500 teachers and officers of the NSW Department of Education enlisted for active service in World War II, leaving their protected occupation to fight and die with distinction in both world wars. In Victoria, in WWII, one in five teachers did not return.

In 1939, at the start of WWII, all unmarried men aged 21 were called up for three months' militia training. They could serve only in Australia or its territories. Conscription was introduced in mid-1942, when all men 18 - 35, and single men aged 35 - 45, joined the Citizens Military Forces (CMF). Teachers not only volunteered for the RAAF, or were conscripted, but were taken for their individual skills, in communications, intelligence, languages and so forth. Older teachers then had a heavier teaching load.

Some schools chose to stay as this letter to the *Sydney Morning Herald* shows:

> Friday January 30, 1942
>
> Sir, In order to remove any misunderstanding which has arisen in the minds of some parents will you allow me to supplement my remarks published in the *Herald* this morning on the subject of evacuation of pupils in certain Church of England schools in or near Sydney? Though the premises recently acquired in the country districts referred to will help to solve the problem in the event of evacuation, becoming necessary, the intention is for work to begin at the Sydney schools and The King's School in the normal way on the dates advertised. There is no intention of immediate evacuation
>
> S M Johnstone, Registrar. Sydney Diocesan Registry.

Stan Gratte's high school at Geraldton was earmarked for an emergency hospital:

> One room contained a lot of stretchers. Another room contained many drums of Chloride of Lime with which to disinfect the expected bodies. The entrance was sandbagged.

Some schools were free to stay, go, rent or buy. If they were in a vulnerable position, and thought that at any tick of the clock bombs could be raining down, they felt very responsible. Some schools had to obey the authorities. The outbreak of war in the Pacific led to the release of *Regulation 35A of the National Security (General) Regulations.* This *Regulation* allowed the Queensland authorities special powers to evacuate school children from their buildings and turn the schools over to the military.

With American and Australian service personnel pouring into Queensland, The Australian Army Hirings Service had the role of locating parks, racecourses and other accommodation to house growing numbers of servicemen. Office accommodation was also in urgent demand for military administration. This information was kept out of the Press.

Lieutenant Melloy was responsible for a smooth transition of property from private ownership to military occupation, with adequate compensation. There was quickly a massive backlog of 700 claims for compensation from some very unhappy local property owners.

One man returned to his Queensland home at the end of the war to find the military had poured concrete into the ground floor of his house over carpets and levelled it. He walked outside and shot himself.

General Blamey's Advanced Land Headquarters were housed at the University of Queensland at St. Lucia. The US 12th Station Hospital arrived in Townsville from Brisbane in March 1942 and requisitioned a street full of 30 houses in Chapman Street at Mysterton Estate for their hospital. Captain Melloy attended a protest meeting of residents. He said Australia was at war and that if the Australian people impeded the Allied Forces in defending our shores and did not cooperate, they would soon be accommodating the enemy. With the arrival of the Americans in Brisbane Captain Melloy was to spend much time liaising with the American Hirings Officer, Major James R Wright, travelling many thousands of miles across North Queensland looking at properties and buildings.

The staff and students of Church of England Boy's School, Toowoomba, were moved eastwards to St. Hilda's School at Southport in April 1942, and their building used as Headquarters for the 1st Australian Army under command of Lieutenant-General Sir John Lavarack. Some other schools acquired in Townsville were St Anne's Church of England Girl's School, St Patrick's (Catholic) College and Townsville Grammar School. Some other schools acquired in Townsville were St Anne's Church of England Girls' School, St Patrick's (Catholic) College and Townsville Grammar School.

The Army Hirings Section took an inventory of the school that they were taking over and carried out an assessment of the school's condition prior to occupation. The School Principal countersigned these documents.

In January 1943 Professor Wright and Dr Hogbin investigated the level of morale amongst the civilian population in Cairns and Townsville, where allied military forces had occupied 177 dwellings. There 90,000 military personnel in Townsville where the civilian population at that time was about 28,000.

In Cairns the Department of Public Instruction decided that schools should remain closed, as the Japanese had made such rapid progress. Many of the children were evacuated.

Tom Hooper:
> I wasn't at school but my brothers and sisters were. We were evacuated to Brisbane. My dad joined up aged 31, I don't know why; he had a reasonable sort of a job.

Cairns Central State School and High School were used for evacuees and missionaries. Cairns North, Parramatta and St Augustine's College were among schools used for personnel or evacuees from New Guinea.

Premier Forgan Smith ordered the immediate closure of coastal schools from Thursday Island to Coolangatta under the *Protection of Persons and Property Order 8A*.

Over the Christmas vacation many NSW parents arranged to evacuate their children from danger zones. Some parents took the initiative and sent their children to boarding schools. Mary O'Byrne was born after the war but knows from family anecdotes that Monica, her mother and her aunt Bernadette and later their younger sister were sent from their home in Dee Why to boarding school at Parramatta, out of harm's way.

Boarding Schools in what were seen as safe areas were inundated with requests from parents. New England Girls' High School had an increase of more than 40, West Armidale Public enrolment was doubled and Armidale High School had a record enrolment. The Demonstration school had a considerable increase, with children from Sydney and one from London. De La Salle College had 180 boarders - a full school, many from Sydney, Newcastle and the coast. Sixteen children boarding at Cotswold were enrolled at Ben Venue, as well as 25 other evacuee children. Armidale PLC had more than double the enrolments from the previous year, with 205 boarders. St Ursula's had a record 90 boarders. At St John's Hostel, Canon Dickens offered part of his home for additional boys. The Church of England Memorial Hostel was full and refusing further applications.

In January 1942, the Armidale branch of National Emergency Services had prepared a complete survey of available housing, with forms asking householders if they preferred adults or children, and which religious denomination. By February 1942, in Armidale, boarding schools and hostels were forced to refuse further applications. Australian actress Queenie Ashton of long-running radio serial *Blue Hills* fame was one of those evacuee mothers arriving with their children on whistling steam trains and by car.

Friday, 27 March, 1942 the *Armidale Express:*

The task of providing accommodation in Armidale for the large number of people, mostly mothers and their children desiring to leave the danger zones in the cities is a difficult one, and the Voluntary Evacuation Committee trying to grapple with the problems urgently needs the willing and active support of all citizens, particularly of those who could take into their homes a mother and child or a mother and two children. Many applications have been received by the Hon, Secretary Archdeacon Forster and it has been possible to satisfactorily place a number of people applying, but the demand for rooms is greatly in excess of the supply offered so far.

Melbourne Grammar School buildings were commandeered by Australian and American forces with some students dispatched to country guest houses.

Chapter 9

The students of SCEGGS, Darlinghurst enthusiastically participated in wartime support work knitting army socks and balaclavas, until they evacuated to Leura, 57 girls at the Chateau Napier guesthouse, declared the food so bad that the students went on strike.

Patricia Berry:
I was only 12 when war broke out. My father was a busy doctor, my mother a nurse. My older sister Judy was studying medicine ... I had three brothers in the war. One was killed in Guinea, when the Beaufort plane he was in blew up because of some dodgy explosives. I was at SCEGGS. When we were evacuated to Leura for about a year. My parents let me go because they had very busy professional lives and they were concerned for my safety. My mother knew two maiden ladies in Leura, and I went to stay with them. When it got cold, they made a tiny fire from sticks and we all crouched over it. I was aware that the Japanese might invade. I was going to meet my mother at Angus and Robertson one day and one of my teachers met me on the way and told me to get off the street and go home because a Japanese reconnaissance plane had flown over.

Sydney Church of England Grammar School, North Sydney bought a house at Mount Victoria for prep to fourth form. Secondary and Prep students at Scots College, Bellevue Hill, would be transferred to Albury Grammar School until a suitable property was acquired. Newington College made standby arrangements with the Methodist College at Orange. Cranbrook School, Bellevue Hill, opened an additional house at Wentworth Falls. Parents had the option of keeping them at the parent school, or sending them to the Falls. Loreto Convent transferred its boarders to Springwood.

By 1942, newspapers were reporting Blue Mountains Schools full of evacuees. The boarders of St Vincent's at Potts Point settled down in Wahgunyah guesthouse, Katoo, 4 kms from the Lithgow munitions factory. The only route back to Sydney was over the Nepean Bridge, so not the most suitable place to retreat to! Another guesthouse, Villers Bret housed the novices. The Katoomba community commented on the plaits which were compulsory in the 1940s. The students made friends, went bushwalking and gave little concerts for the community.

The Royal Far West Children's Home, Drummond House at Manly had 178 country children aged 0–12 years with medical problems. They were relocated to Springwood during 1942 and 1943 and their premises occupied by the Australian Women's Army Service.

Goulburn was another very popular spot. *Goulburn Evening Post*, 4 February 1942: 'Although the majority of children came from Sydney and suburbs, and Wollongong, several children from Queensland, New Guinea and even Hong Kong have enrolled at this centre. Many children have moved to country areas such as Goulburn to live with relatives etc., but some from the coastal areas have fathers training with the Light Horse Regiment and they have temporarily settled here.'

Margaret Taylor, who lived in a house on forty acres across the road from Bishopthorpe remembers the St Gabriel girls walking to school in a long line of two, hand in hand, known as a 'crocodile', over a mile to have lessons at the PLC, as she rode by them on her bike, waving. Margaret attended the Presbyterian Ladies College as a day pupil, but it was primarily a boarding school drawing pupils from the Riverina to the Snowy Mountains. She writes:

A friend Jean from the Riverina was booked to go to PLC in Pymble, but as the war worsened, her parents opted for PLC in Goulburn instead. Another friend Heather, had cousins evacuated from their inner Sydney suburb to live with them. Girls from farming families who had been sent to Sydney schools were brought back to the Goulburn area. Numerous girls who were day pupils at Sydney schools were sent to board. My main recollection is of St Gabriel's College, Waverley, coming and being accommodated at the old Bishopsthorpe. The monks there had been transferred or joined the armed services as chaplains. With clothing rationing, nobody could insist on school uniforms being correct and we became quite a mixture of colours, patterns and tartans.

The papers reported two girls, whose father was a miner in New Guinea, had arrived with their mother in Goulburn.

Chapter 9

Jacqueline Parker went to Bathurst as a boarder:

> I am now 79 years old and was sent to a country Boarding School
> from my fee paying school in 1942 after the submarines came
> into Sydney Harbour, together with my sister, who was seven
> years older. I asked my mother why we were going and she said,
> 'Because it's safe'. Our mother was a cutter at Central Station. My
> sister never forgave my mother for sending her away. She hated
> the restrictions - like they always read your letters before they
> were sent. She reckoned mum just wanted to go to work and have
> us looked after. My sister was 14 at the time and only spent one
> year there. I was seven and spent three years there. The Boarding
> School was at Perthville, just outside Bathurst and it is still there,
> not as a school, but still has boarders there. It belongs to the Black
> Sisters of St. Joseph. It was the first time they took Sydney girls
> there as it had country girls only till then and we were always
> known as the Sydney girls. There were about 15 of us and we met
> up at Central Station and travelled together. We had three pieces
> of fruit a week - we had to write our name on a paper bag for the
> fruit. We had to eat everything that was put before us. It was not
> an unhappy experience, but I definitely missed my family and was
> happy when I was allowed to come home permanently.

Another major move was that of Scots College to the property Karralee,
Bathurst. During 1941-42, air raid shelters were constructed to
accommodate 600 persons, at a cost of £1,460. They were soon in use
and they relocated, the new property eventually becoming Scots School
Bathurst. A hundred old boys were now in the military, with twenty-
seven killed and another forty missing or prisoners of war. Schoolboys
turned quickly into servicemen as many of the sixth form left the College
only to enlist for the war. There were twenty changes to staff during this
time, they either served in the forces, or helped with war work, ranging
from electrical installations to interpreting German films.

King's School, at first facing the possibility of the school buildings being
requisitioned, obtained Tudor House at Moss Vale, for their prep school.

Pupils at Shore College, North Sydney had a remarkable experience.
The school is high up, near the Harbour - a lovely setting, but vulnerable.

A Carefree War

In December 1941, Shore School Council decided much to parent's relief to purchase a branch school for Juniors well outside of Sydney. The Headmaster inspected properties from Yass to Katoomba and decided on a two storey hotel at Mount Victoria, previously a hostel for Lithgow munitions factory workers, for £6,500 (a pub with no beer). There was concern about faulty electrical wiring and old plumbing, because if there was something dangerous, small boys would find it and there was a lot of hard work to get it opened in February 1942, when 83 pupils and 75 boarders moved in, with every bed occupied.

The boys made their beds and cleaned their rooms. Cold showers were taken daily, with a hot bath weekly. Clean shoes were encouraged and when the local paper shop suddenly obtained a supply of Kiwi Boot Polish, it was inundated with boys.

A haircut meant cycling 5 kms to Blackheath, even in winter. The whole school ran 1.4 kms daily before classes. The boys walked in a crocodile every Sunday to St Peter's Church and provided the choir. They fought with the local public school boys, and won. Pocket money went on sausage rolls for a penny halfpenny, sausage rolls threepence at Mrs March's tuckshop. The boys sang 'We like Mrs March's Apple Pies' to the tune of Colonel Bogey, much to everyone's delight. They slid down hills on pieces of tin and everyone caught measles. (An extra nurse had to be employed!).

Jim White:

> I have broken my glasses while playing with sledges ... one boy would get on his bike and tow the sledge down the hill. When he got up enough speed, he would try and tip the boy on the sledge off. Once I turned two summersaults and nearly busted my neck.

Boys rode their bikes over an 'assault course', and to Little Hartley to buy apples, or to Mount Victoria Falls. They played cricket, went bush walking and rock climbing (with just a rope), picked blackberries, swam, competed in athletics, explored Jenolan Caves, played French cricket, marbles and saddle-m-nag. They shot rabbits with their rifles and sold the skins. Some Saturdays, they visited Blackheath cinema to see a film; *Johnny Edgar* and *Sweater Girl* were favourites.

Chapter 9

Robert Goldrick:

My skills at billiards improved with ready access to the table at the hotel where we stayed, and my physical fitness was at an all time high because there were no motor cars.

James Bretherton and Jim Creer:

In mid-winter, our beds along with others were located on the first floor veranda. To keep warm in bed, we fought to see which one of us could 'win' a threadbare carpet to cover us to supplement the two issued blankets. It was so cold some nights we went to bed dressed in our uniforms over our pyjamas plus football socks.

Michael Pringle:

A standout activity of the school was a bushwalk. Lunch was a chop or sausage cooked over a fire, a hunk of bread and an apple, while somebody boiled a billie for tea. I recall at least two hikes down to the floor of the Jamieson Valley, and the hike back up, which left one's legs aching. On one of those trips, lunch was by a billabong. Before swimming, the older boys had to kill a red bellied black snake so it wouldn't share the cool water with us. The snake was then tossed onto an anthill.

John Valder:

One of the really great joys of being at Mt Victoria was that the school was practically on the busy main western line. We quickly became authorities on all the different types of steam locomotives. A more sombre memory I have is of us lining the Great Western Highway to applaud and encourage the young soldiers marching all the way from Bathurst to Sydney on their way to active service (and death in some cases). I can still hear the sound of hundreds of army boots hitting the bitumen.

Ian Curlewis watched his father sail away in the *Queen Mary*. His mother and grandparents decided to move up to Leura, where his grandparents had cottages. He attended the Shore School for a term and then civilian fears of invasion subsided. His parents and grandparents moved back to Sydney but he stayed on as a boarder. He stayed for two terms, went back to stay with an aunt in Bellevue Hill and the Japanese submarine shelled Rose Bay. The shells must have gone right over his aunt's roof.

The boys seemed contented with their lot.

Peter Raleigh:

> One very memorable ride was down Victoria Pass and across to Lithgow. As we climbed the hills out of Lithgow, we came across a anti-aircraft battery and we boys were most impressed. These guns were there to protect the small arms factory in Lithgow, where the .303 rifles were made for our troops. School assembly was held across the road from the main building. During winter, the ground was frozen hard so each morning we all ran around the block to keep warm.

Peter Valder:

> We had free access to the local shops and walking up to the post office and general store on the Great Western Highway. It was always interesting to look at the local dingo pups and other native animals kept at a small zoo on the corner opposite the Imperial Hotel.

Ross Playfair:

> Our family lived at Blaxland on the lower Blue Mountains at the time, so we did not go to Mount Victoria to avoid any possible Japanese attacks, but rather to enjoy the lifestyle and the environment. Unfortunately we only had one snowfall during the year, but we made the most of it. My close friend, Roger Jefferson and I considered ourselves the bicycle specialists and checked the bearings and lubricated the other bikes and tried to adjust bent wheels etc.

The boys dutifully wrote home to their mothers. Here are two letters from 'Geoff', (with his spelling intact):

Dear mum,

Yesterday there was a big mist and you couldn't see two hundred away. Boyd fell off his bike and broke his arm. Don't send any comics, for Mr

Anderson said we were not aloud to have them. Ted has got swollen glans. We have sport today. We play on the colflinks or down the main road to a pitch which is about one mile away. Our holidays begin on 1st April to the 9th and I will be coming up to Amaroo. Please tell me Gran's address.

love Geoff

Dear mum,

We had a blackout last night. My choclats did not melt in the train and I have only had to or three so far. My heels are better. I have bought a lote of books. We went down to a cricet pitch yesterday and had a game. I would much rather be at Amaroo than at school. We have great fun watching trains. It is raining today and we can't go outside. I do not want my paints. The food is OK.

Love Geoff

None of the boys regretted the years they spent in their mountain retreat.

And Guy Fitzharding was very proud of the fact that he had gone to school in a public bar!

Chapter 10

Handkerchiefs and No Pets
–The Evacuation of Torres Strait Islands, Northern Territory and Queensland

My mother was terrified that a Japanese parachutist would come down near our farm while she was alone there.

– Mary Ford, in Queensland

Chapter 10

Prime Minister Mr Curtin stated, 'The time has gone by for argument. The instructions of the Federal Government must be carried out.'

On 22 March, 1942, nine Mitsubishi G4M1 'Betty' bombers of the Japanese Navy's Tokao Kokutai, 23rd Koku Sentai circled over Katherine, disappeared, and returned to drop about ninety-one 60 kgs bombs. Eighty-four of these bombs were anti-personnel 'Daisy Cutters'. Damage to planes at Katherine was minimal, but some Aboriginals were unfortunately killed. The special threat to Northern Australia by the Japanese from late 1941 resulted in the formation of several Aboriginal and Torres Strait Islander Units such as the Torres Strait Light Infantry Battalion. Irregular units like the 21st North Australia Observer Unit, based at Katherine, utilised local knowledge and skills of local Aboriginals. Thursday Island, 39 kilometres north of Cape York Peninsula was evacuated.

Stella Sun:

> I was ten years old when we had to leave, and I feel guilty because I enjoyed it and felt it was an adventure. The women and children all left by boat. The islanders stood and sang *The Thursday Island Song* and we threw handkerchiefs with pennies wrapped in them for them to wipe their tears. We had to evacuate from Thursday Island in January 1942, as it was the military headquarters for the Torres Strait and a base for Australian and American forces. It had been our home since my grandfather came out in the 1880s as a pearling pioneer. He eventually returned to China and we took over his shop. My aunt brought up nine children there. Residents of Japanese origin or descent were interned. The residents did not return until after the end of the war and many ethnic Japanese were repatriated. The island was not bombed, maybe because it was the burial place of Japanese pearl shell divers, or possibly as there were Japanese residents on the island. Nearby Horn Island was heavily bombed. The Queensland government commandeered ships for evacuation. We were given half a day's notice. Luckily we had an uncle who stayed behind and looked after everything. He bought up the discarded army equipment and sold it back to them.

A Carefree War

The Arnhem Land Region, around 500 kms from Darwin, unmapped land with resident Aboriginals, was feared a possible Japanese landing site. Japanese navy personnel had enquired about Aboriginals being used as a workforce in the past.

Alice Springs, the third largest town in the Northern Territory, in the geographic centre of Australia, remained under civilian administration. The army took control of stock routes and bores on routes were increased and a meatworks and a piggery built to provide food for defence personnel in the Territory.

In Darwin, Aboriginal women were evacuated but about 20 per cent of Aboriginal men, employed by the armed forces as woodcutters or at Fanny Bay jail, stayed. The last ship, the MV *Koolama*, hot and crowded, left on Sunday, 15 February, 1942 and later sank after attacks by Japanese aircraft. (There was an alleged mutiny resulting from these attacks).

The Army was responsible for Darwin's evacuees, but no clear plan was given. The place was a hotbed of rumour, the road south soon crammed with every kind of vehicle, wheels stirring up red dust. Queensland banks, from Cooktown to the border, had records copied and sent out west.

Audrey Gross:
> My father was Manager of the Bank of New South Wales in Cooktown, from about 1938 until the bank was closed in about 1941. Most people were encouraged to leave Cape York. We ended up on the Sunshine Coast. Whether we were moved because of Bank or Federal Government policy I do not know. We had a car, and would have travelled at least to Cairns, however the Hayles boats were a big means of going to Cairns where we used to travel by coastal ships to Townsville and Brisbane. The *Manunda* and *Manora* were two ships that we used. I believe the Aboriginals on Hopevale, a Lutheran Mission, were sent to Cherburg, near Murgon. It wasn't until about 1960s that they were able to return to their homelands.

In *Australia under Attack*, Douglas Lockwood describes how his newly married wife wanted to stay with him and applied for an 'essential' job -

she became an army typist. The author writes, 'Fortunately she became convinced of the wisdom of leaving one week before the first raid.'

When the bombing started the civilian population was given half an hour to collect a few belongings and leave the town in brake vans. Stockingless, with their tin hats, they left their homes and treasures, carrying parcels of food and blankets against the desert air. The first two nights, myriads of mosquitoes attacked them. They went to the railway terminal at Birdum, 300 miles south of Darwin, and were put in army trucks. The party passed through the Tennant Creek goldfield the following day, camping near an overland telegraph station - a distance of more than 200 miles, eventually reaching Alice Springs.

Breakfast for the whole trainload at Quorn was prepared by the Country Women's Association. 'It was a wonderful meal—real sausages, butter, and fresh fruit' said Mrs. McManus, a passenger. 'The Red Cross was there to help us too, and my treat after nearly nine days was a hair wash, while the children were given baths.' They eventually reached Adelaide by special train. Among the evacuees were oil company employees from Dutch New Guinea, who had come to Darwin in a Catalina flying boat, and a Government official's wife from the island of Dobo, Indonesia, with three young, children, which they heard had been bombed.

On page 56 in the report *Plans for Air Raid Precautions and Evacuation of Civilians, Darwin* police stated there were 1,066 women and 900 children. In 2,500 leaflets distributed to households on 15 December, 1941, rules for compulsory civilian evacuation were printed, without indication as to when this might happen or who would be evacuated. The Army advised an evacuation of 822 on the SS *Zealandia*, army transport and under their control. The first group of 225 left aboard the general cargo and passenger ship, *Koolunga*. A batch of 530 evacuees left Darwin on the SS *Zealandia* on 20 December, 1941. Stories circulated that the ship had not been cleaned for months, food and water were short and toilet and washing facilities inadequate. According to Peter Grose in *An Awkward Truth*, the *Adelaide News* got the story but it was censored. Pets were ordered to be destroyed, but not chickens, which could be a food source. An eight litre water bag per family, two blankets and one small calico bag containing personal items and one suitcase not exceeding 35 pounds was all that was allowed. Guards threw overweight bags overboard. Some on the *Zealandia* cabins were designed for four people, but held 11. The ship took on 200 Japanese internees at Thursday Island. Patricia Ayre was one of the few to see Japanese POWs:

> When I was seven, I was evacuated from Darwin on the SS *Zealandia* with my mother and younger sister. The ship was blacked out at night. One night, I was slow getting back to our cabin and a sailor grabbed me and pushed me inside but not before I saw Japanese POWs, who had been marched up from the hold to get hosed down. We were allowed one suitcase between the three of us. One night we had to get on our lifejackets and assemble on deck. A ship had gone by without signalling, but it was alright. For the whole trip we ate tinned Camp Pie. On Christmas Day, they had plates of mince in the Mess. I was the only one there - everyone else was seasick. I had three plates full. Looking back, I think it must have been the Pie minced up! Mum was very good but years later, she told me how frightened she was. Somewhere along the east coast, my sister became very sick and mother went ashore to find a chemist and get something for her. Coming back, some drunken sailors pretended to help her but took the bag and threw it in the ocean. Mother got back onboard safely and my sister eventually recovered. We were taken to Melbourne, where we spent two nights on the floor of the Town Hall, and then to Adelaide and the Mount Lofty Ranges. We returned to Darwin after the war. The *Zealandia* was sunk in air raids on February 19, 1942, and we lost our house in the bombing. After the war, I was talking to an aboriginal girl and she said she and her friends were put in trucks and evacuated to Alice Springs.

The SS *Zealandia* had served as a troopship in both world wars, transporting the ill-fated Australian 8th Division. During the February 1942 air raids, Japanese planes attacked *Zealandia*. The order was given to abandon ship. *Zealandia* sank, leaving only her masts clear.

The *Cairns Post Advertiser* described how the war disrupted lives in

Chapter 10

Northern Queensland. On 6 February, 1942, four thousand women and children moved to safer places in the country after offers of assistance under the state government's voluntary evacuation scheme.

Not a House Left. A newspaper article declared, 'Few Country Homes Vacant.'

> The demand for houses in Stanthorpe started a month ago with the result that today there is not a home to let. Many strangers have arrived in the town, and the schools promise to be overflowing. In Warwick, because of the influx of women and children, house rentals are soaring. Pittsworth residents have agreed to 'put up' as many people as possible. Allora is prepared to take 200 or 300 people, and ways and means are being devised. Clifton has about 20 evacuees from Brisbane, most of whom are staying with relatives. Goondiwindi has received a few inquiries; steps are being taken to shelter as many people as possible, if necessary. Glen Innes has welcomed about 200 people from Sydney and Newcastle, and a few from Brisbane.

Fiddes Skardon, miner and drover tried to enlist with a friend but they were cane farmers and needed on the land '... if the Japs invaded and the war came, we always thought we'd go guerrilla. I'd bought a .22 calibre rifle in Cairns with 1,000 round of ammo and of course I had all the horses and packs. We could hide in the hills.'

Babinda and Tully, near Cairns annually compete for the Golden Gumboot award for Australia's wettest town. Babinda is usually the winner, recording an annual rainfall of over 4,200 millimetres. In 1942, it was a ghost town after evacuation.

Mary Ford:
> I was evacuated from Tully, Queensland, 140 kms south of Cairns, when I was nine years old, to the Darling Downs, where we didn't know people. My sister, aged 17, my mother and I went. My father stayed as he was in essential services. We just had time to grab basic luggage - there were police in the crowd at the station. I don't know how everybody knew it was time to go because not many people had a telephone at home. It was early February 1942.

A Carefree War

We all knew we were in a war zone. The Brisbane Line was generally understood to mean that the northern part of Australia would be surrendered to invaders, although it was never spelt out, only accredited to Robert Menzies and Arthur Faddon, and referred to once by General McArthur. A lot of the men had gone to fight and guns had been requisitioned after Dunkirk and sent to England. We felt very vulnerable, although the speed with which the Japanese took Singapore and the bombing of Pearl Harbour surprised everybody. We lived up a hill, next to jungle and my mother was terrified that a Japanese parachutist would come down near us.

We had been wearing camouflaged cloaks to school for some time, and were given cotton wool balls for our ears and bits of rubber tubing to bite on if bombs exploded. School hours were staggered – 8 am to lunchtime, and 11 am to 4 pm. There were often Japanese planes zooming about. Once, on the way back home from school I was caught in an air raid warning. I was frightened and did not know whether to continue on home or go back to school. I decided school, being on flat ground was the better option and scampered back, in the noise of the *ack-ack* guns, throwing myself into a slit trench in the school grounds.

My mother was not happy on the Darling Downs and we were one of the first families to return home. In May, I remember the boom of the guns in the Battle of the Coral Sea.

Schooldays at the beginning of the 1940s were punctuated by air raid sirens and practice drills, students sent running to trenches, crouching low, pulling their brown and green capes over their heads with pegs between their teeth in case of a bomb blast.

David Tranter, who lived at Eacham on the Atherton Tablelands remembers the troops:

Early in 1943, I was packed off to boarding school at Charters Towers. Innisfail Railway Station was packed with Australian soldiers and when I came home, I learned that the Atherton Tablelands had become a vast military encampment.

Chapter 10

Hellen Bradshaw:

I lived in East Innisfail with my parents and my brother. In 1941, he was sixteen and I was eight. My father was in an essential service and a volunteer ambulance driver. A friend of his was driving to Brisbane and my father was anxious to get us out of the area because of a Japanese invasion seeming imminent in North Queensland. We could go to my mother's sister, Aunt Jess. It took ten days to get there on dirt roads, without bridges, (we had to drive through creeks, clutching our suitcases). The road signs were down and we continually got lost. When we arrived late at a little township, Miriam Vale, 464 kms north of Brisbane on the Bruce Highway, we booked into the local hotel and during the night cowboys arrived on their horses and were drinking under our windows. Mother and I went for a shower in a tin shed separate from the hotel and our driver came and said, 'Get out of there quickly!' The owner was peering in at us. I don't remember my brother and I being frightened at all - I don't know about mum.

Hilary Walker:

Our family was evacuated from a sugar cane farm outside Gordonvale in North Queensland in February 1942. Advice to evacuate was first given by a local policeman. We did not go. An order to evacuate was later delivered by the local policeman and we did go. My parents chose to go to a remote corner of the Atherton Tableland, close enough for my father to be able to continue farming. We set out in a truck with some furniture. Mother, father, three children and the neighbour's young girl. The drive up to the Tableland involved careful timing, as we had to go up to the Gillies Highway, which was a one way gravel road with a speed limit of 10 mph. We had to be at the bottom gate at a set time, and then leave in a convoy of vehicles. Number plates and time of entrance were noted and telephoned to the top gate. Vehicles were checked out at the top gate and times noted. One hour was allowed for the trip and if a vehicle came out sooner, they could be fined for breaking the speed limit. If they did not arrive, a search party was sent out, as many vehicles went over the side. The final part of the journey was along a track full of sticky, red mud. We had arrived at Topaz, a small community of dairy farmers, almost cut off from the outside world.

There was no electricity or running water and only one party line for the telephones. Our house was really a shack that had been uninhabited for some time, and infested with fleas that blackened our legs. I remember the copper being boiled and the water being poured all over the floor and lime being sprinkled on under the building. That took a lot of hop out of the fleas. Every house in this district that I visited had fleas. We more or less settled in with my young brother, who was about five months old, hanging from the rafters in his cane bassinet, just out of flea hopping distance. I enrolled in the local one teacher school on 9 February, 1942, and Ethel, who had come with us, a few days later. The school was on high stumps with shelter underneath, which was useful as it seemed to rain nearly every day. A horse paddock was next to the grounds. Children either walked or came on horse. Some horses arrived with a sugar bag on their back, plus two or three children. I found the children daunting. They were serious and shabby, and of course had no shoes. Of course they were different from the children I had previously been to school with. These were marginal farms with parents struggling to make a living. Many of the children would be up before dawn to help with the milking, which was all done by hand, and then home for the second milking after school. I found that Mr Fischer, the teacher, did most of the teaching late in the day as quite a few of the pupils dozed off in the morning.

There is always plenty of simple amusement in the bush. We used to take a sugar bag into the rainforest, then called the 'scrub', and collect purple passion fruit that then grew wild. Closer to home, we caught interesting things. I can remember catching a centipede which we somehow chopped up and put in a billy. Much to our fascination, it was still marching. There were plenty of black snakes, which we did not catch. Our connection with the nearest town was the cream truck, which came twice a week to collect the cream and take it to the butter factory. The milk was separated in hand turned separators and had to maintain a certain speed to work. When the operator reached a correct speed, a bell would ding. This speed had to be maintained with the regular dinging keeping the operator at it. The cream was put into metal containers ready for pick up. There was no refrigeration to keep the cream cool, but the butter from the local factory was fine. The skimmed milk was put into containers and fed to pigs. I remember great blobs of solid sour milk being poured into the troughs.

We stayed for six months and it was memorable, and as time went by, I was able to appreciate how tough the living was for these farmers. At the same time it was a tight knit community. There was a community hall where local dances were held and a couple of tennis courts that were much used.

In Brisbane, by day the river bustled with merchant shipping and small naval craft. At night children, peered from behind blackout curtains at Australian warships and US submarines returning or departing. Children became quick at identifying Beauforts, Wirraways, Tiger Moths, Kittyhawks, and Flying Fortresses in the bright blue Brisbane skies.

Alan Galwey:
I was only five when the war broke out. Father, who had put his age up had survived WWI and Gallipoli, and as an old soldier, he was aware of what war was all about. We left Brisbane and rented a house at Toowoomba, my brother, myself and our parents. It was alongside a railway and we watched the troop trains coming and going. Mother baked apple pies and took them out to the trains for the soldiers to say thank you. My father got a job at the butter factory and we stayed about eighteen months. I was the youngest and to me everything was a game, I didn't appreciate the danger. I remember the family driving into Toowoomba and having the most delicious scones and jam from the Red Cross.

A Carefree War

Ian Murray Wilson:

I was about eight when the war started. We all thought the Japs were going to invade and I was aware of the chance of being killed. My Dad joined the army, but he never left Australia, he was too old really. He was a clerk at Dalgety's and helped break the wharfies strike. He stayed in Brisbane. Mum and I and my sister went up to Dalby, about two hundred kilometres from Brisbane, to Mr and Mrs Marshall, dairy farmers on the rich soil of the Darling Downs. They had a place between Dalby and Tipton. I took my fox terrier, Mackie. One of my jobs in the morning was to wash the mud off the cow's udders, ready for milking. I had lovely warm water, the cows didn't like cold! We went to a one teacher school about a mile and a half down a gravel road. I was running along the road by myself and I jumped over a hollow log, looked down and there was a snake in it. I ran along in the air like they do in the Tom and Jerry cartoons. We got on very well with the Marshalls and kept in touch with them until they passed away. I'm not sure how my parents found their farm. I think the authorities arranged it. We had an air raid shelter in Brisbane. Mrs Dunn next door had a much fancier one.

W.B. (Bill) Martin:

During the bad days of WWII, I was a child in Townsville. My uncle, Captain Greenwood was the Port Superintendent in Darwin. He had lots of trips to Canberra, Sydney. He advised my family to get out of Townsville, as the Japs had said they were going to sterilise all the males and breed with the females and in three generations all the white blood would be neutralised.

The Brisbane Line was an overwhelming fear in North Queensland. So I was sent to live in Brisbane with my aunt, Mrs C E Cox at Oriel Road, Clayfield, Brisbane. At the time, I was attending the Ascot State School. Owing to the shortage of school teachers, we only attended school for half a day. One day, my cousin, Harry Cox and I had to take my cousin Leslie's lunch to school, as she had forgotten it. It was quite a step to the Clayfield College, where she was a student. On our way to the college, every air raid siren in Brisbane sounded off. Harry and I ran for our lives to the school. Ladies on their front steps called to us to run as the Japs were coming. Two little kids running for their lives! When we got to the school, all the kids and teachers were in a huge air raid shelter under the school, lit by hurricane lamps. The girls were singing to keep their spirits up. It was the day of the Battle of the Coral Sea, which we won and saved Australia from invasion. Some say they had no intention of attacking Australia. If so, how come they had invasion money printed to be used by the Australian people after they had taken over.

My aunt had an air raid shelter under their house, as most people did at the time. The air raid shelter was full of food in case of an invasion. Most afternoons, Harry and I would raid the shelter and pinch tins of condensed milk, tins of sardines, bully beef, etc. to snack on. When the war was over, Auntie Lottie said we had better get the food out of the shelter. No tins where left. Harry and I were in strife over that. Auntie Lottie 'said' what would have happened if the Japs had invaded.

A Reverend Rix declared in the *Morning Bulletin*, April 1946, (and this was widely reported), that it was by a miracle that when the Japanese invasion was threatening in 1941 it was the driest Queensland season in the memory of both white and black man, thereby enabling the Americans to build runways for attack in the decisive Battle of the Coral Sea.

Rear-Admiral G C Muirhead-Gould, formerly officer in charge of the naval establishment in Sydney, at a Press conference at the British Ministry of Information in London, August 1943, claimed that allied sea power saved Australia from invasion. He said that the Japanese did not attack Australia probably for the same reason that Hitler did not invade Britain after the fall of France, and that both Tojo and Hitler, despite the great victories that they had won, had not destroyed allied sea power and they knew that if they stuck their necks out too far allied sea power would defeat them eventually. He asserted vigorously that

Australians should become more sea-minded and should never forget that their very existence depended on the British Empire's control of sea communications.

> I hope that Australians realise ' what a weighty decision had to be made in the Admiralty in London to provide the great liners that brought their troops back from the Middle East and what vital sacrifices had to be made in other theatres to provide supplies, equipment, and ships and all other material which enabled those magnificent Diggers to meet the Japanese on equal terms in New Guinea and to impose on the Japanese the first resounding defeat that they had suffered.
>
> We could never have accomplished all that if we had lost-control of the sea. The Japanese could at that time always produce a locally superior fleet, but sea power did not depend on far-flung fleets but on the British Battle Fleet. Tojo had every reason to fear The British fleet. Australians must become sea-minded. They live on the most wonderful sea in the world - the Pacific and the New South Wales coast is one of the most beautiful on which to live. The sea is all round them and in future they must show their pride by all-out support of their Navy.

Bob Taylor and his sister Joyce lived at Trebonne, a small township, about 100 km north of Townsville:

> North Queensland. My father, also Bob, together with my mother Matilda, owned a typical country store and during the war, Dad was the local Air Raid Precautions (ARP) Warden, one of 51 in the Shire. I understand he was exempt from military service, because he owned a store, but a brother served in the AIF in the Middle East. My mother's sister Ann Boyd lived in Townsville with her husband, Percy, running a boarding house, so Percy was also exempt from service, but an ARP Warden in Townsville. They had had two children Joan and Eric. His brother also served in the AIF in the ME where he was killed.
>
> During 1942, the area north of Mackay had been declared a war zone, I was seven, my sister six, Joan ten and Eric nine and our parents decided to evacuate us to Richmond, western Queensland,

where our mothers were born, to live with our grandmother and three spinster aunts. Four of Gran's sons had enlisted, two in the AIF (one in the ME) and two in the RAAF. Ann Boyd and her children went first in early 1942, but Ann returned to Townsville to help with the boarding house. Shortly after, my mother, Joyce and I joined the Boyd children, but Mum stayed on for a while before returning to Trebonne.

My sister and I spent about six months in Richmond, but the Boyd's stayed longer and their mother visited them occasionally during their almost twelve months away. We four attended the Richmond State School across the road from Gran's, and whilst I do not remember much about this period, I vividly remember the flies!!! To enter the classroom, two students had to do duty on the screen door, brushing flies off each child before slamming the door shut after each one. I do not remember much of the time spent at Richmond, but I do not ever recall being frightened. We were pampered by Gran and our aunts, and it really was one big wonderful experience.

Gordon McFadden, (Don):

I was 13 years old at the time of the Pacific War, living with my parents, who had a plumbing business in Queensland, and unlike other evacuees, I was sent from the bush to the coast. The only time I remember being scared was when war was declared in Europe. My parents were away on holiday and coming back by ship and I was thinking they could get torpedoed! At home we had a big map, six feet by four, and we'd sit around the crackling short wave radio and put pins in where the battles were. We were always looking for petrol permits. At Toowoomba, the country boys brought food rationing coupons in because they didn't need them and swopped them for clothing coupons.

My father was a Captain in the Voluntary Defence Corps. His job was to blow up the bridges in his area if the Japanese invaded. Ammunition was stacked ready. My mother was busy running the plumbing business. Our employees fixed the pipes in ships damaged in the war. We never knew when they would be coming or going and we'd get calls in the night to pick up employees. My dad went over t Stradbroke Island with two mates to defuse three incendiary bombs on the beach. One exploded, killing one of them and dad was badly burned. Downlands RC School had been evacuated and taken over by the American Army for a hospital and he walked across the paddocks to get there for treatment.

I was sent to Toowoomba Boys Prep School for one term and then the army took it over. The girls at St Hilda's in Southport were sent to Warwick and our lot was sent to Southport. So they got the girls out and left the boys to take the flak! Many a time the sirens went over Brisbane and there were no Japanese planes, and the Japanese planes flew over and there were no sirens! We had trenches at Southport and were drilled at a signal to stand, push in our two pupil benches and march to the trenches. The first time the warning went, the boys fled to the trenches, jumping over verandas and each other in their eagerness, getting there in record time.

On Wednesday, 8 January, 1947, Brigid Richmond aged 13 wrote to the *Sydney Morning Herald:*

I used to live up at Brisbane until last December and in February 1941, when I was eight years old, our schools were all shut up because of the war. The Trades and Labour Council decided to evacuate some children to the country, with women to look after them. I was one of the children who went. We had many good times, such as picnics in a pine forest.

Bruce Crawford was intrigued that he and his brother were sent north of the Brisbane Line,

My father Harold Crawford OBE, VRD had obtained a commission in the Royal Australian Navy Reserve in 1927. At the outbreak of WWII, he held the rank of Lieutenant Commander. As he was proficient in Italian, he was called up in the phony war period to Naval Intelligence, serving as Naval Intelligence Officer Torres Strait, at Darwin, the Philippines and Japan.

Chapter 10

With the call up, my mother moved back to my mother's parent's home situated on the corner of Mark Street and Elystan Road, New Farm, Brisbane. For reasons never explained to me, my elder brother David and I were sent to Biggenden in the Northern Burnett district of Maryborough. Our mother accompanied us and as an uncle was then living in Biggenden, I presumed we lived with him. Why we were sent north of Brisbane is a bit of a mystery. No doubt in Naval Intelligence there would have been considerable discussion about the Brisbane Line. New Farm was in the direct bombing line. The assumption was, if Brisbane was bombed, the Japanese aircraft would come up the Brisbane River, bombing the shipping wharves on the Teneriffe and New Farm reaches. The United States navy had their submarine base with mother ships moored off Macquarie Street, New Farm. Aircraft would proceed to the New Farm power house, the major power supply for Brisbane at that time, cross New Farm to the Story Bridge and the city centre. During the war, opposite our house in Elystan Road, was the WRAAF hostel and across the road in Oxlade Drive was the USA navy officer's club, known as 'Riverside'. I do not know when we returned to New Farm. The uncle in Biggenden joined the RAAF. I presume the return was after the Battle of the Coral Sea, when things stabilised. We also had a sand-bagged air raid shelter under our home at New Farm, which survived until the 1950s.

Not every household was lucky enough to have the luxury of an air raid shelter close to their home. These shelters in the backyards were usually a deep trench covered by a corrugated water tank cut in half and covered in sandbags. For women who were fortunate to have one it was a constant reminder that bombs might fall from the sky as she hung her washing in the sunshine.

With the Allied successes, the danger from Japanese occupation receded and most of the students were back home by February 1943. The air raid shelters however continued to silently provide escape in Australian backyards.

Chapter 11
Staying with Friends

Often and often we talk with gratitude of your Mum and Dad in taking Aileen and the boys in 1942. It was a great relief to me to know that whatever happened to Sydney – and perhaps to me – they at least were as far away from trouble as was humanly possible, and in very good hands.

– Max Craymer to Stella (nee Pfeiffer) on death
of her mother 13 May, 1974

Chapter 11

If there were no relatives in Australia, desperate parents turned to friends.

Ann (Vernon) Gray was evacuee from Double Bay:

My family lived in Double Bay and I was at school at Ascham in Edgecliff. I don't know whether the school was closed down in May - June, 1942, but I do remember air raid drills being practised with all the little girls lying down on the floor of the washroom of the preparatory school and my father and his friends digging an air raid shelter in the garden at home. My parents were friends with Dulcie and Everett Magnus who lived in the next street and I was close in age (five and three quarters) and in the same class at Ascham as their daughter Judith. Dulcie came from Armidale originally and her mother Mrs Hutton, always known to us as Huttie, still lived there. At this stage many of the Ascham boarders had either gone home to the country and were being tutored by Ascham via correspondence, or had been moved with some teachers to properties out of Sydney.

I assume that my parents and the Magnus family talked together and decided that it would be also safer to send Judith and me to the country – Judith to her grandmother Huttie and me to Cam and Myra Howard who were friends of Huttie's and lived nearby. Cam Howard taught at the Armidale Teachers' College, in the Music Department, I was later told. Interestingly, I have no memories of the journey from Sydney to Armidale, of meeting the Howards and their sons Graham and David, nor of the departure of my parents (or perhaps just of my mother). I had been used to staying for periods of several days with my grandfather and great-aunts at Roseville, so perhaps the idea of an extended 'sleep-over' without my family didn't worry me as much as it would worry many small children. Memories I do have are: The Howard's house, which was brick with an entry porch approached up several steps, and with a smallish front lawn surrounded by a tall, clipped cypress hedge. I particularly remember the cypress hedge as Graham (who was the same age as I was) and I had a hidey-hole underneath it into which we could retreat after having occasionally reduced poor Myra Howard to tears with our bad behaviour. Graham and I and Judith Magnus all went to the Armidale Public School. Presumably I usually walked there and back with Graham, but I distinctly remember one day when I must have arrived home after school before Graham. I went back to look down the street after hearing a loud wailing coming nearer and nearer. It was Graham who was tearing down the street pursued by an angry nesting magpie. I learnt to avoid the magpie nesting trees after that. I have no memory of the school buildings or of other children there, with the exception of one girl (name unknown) who invited Judith Magnus and me to come home with her after school. We walked and walked along a dusty road right out into the country (it seemed to me) and finally arrived to be greeted by the girl's mother who sent us straight back to our homes in town.

Presumably there were no telephone calls possible, because when Judith and I arrived back at her Grandmother Huttie's house, no-one was at home to greet us. We sat contentedly on a large box outside (perhaps a meter box) and Huttie finally arrived home furious. She and poor Myra Howard had been out searching the streets for us. I can only appreciate now, after having been responsible for my own children and their various friends, just how worried they must have been. My final memory is being in the Armidale Hospital with measles. It seems I was sent there because my family wanted to ease Myra Howard's task of caring for her own family and for an extra sick child. My memory is not of being sick, nor of the hospital surrounds, but of my mother coming from Sydney to visit me and bringing with her the Disney comic book of *Dumbo*, the Flying Elephant. What joy! I have no idea how long I was with the Howards in Armidale. It may have only been two or three months as I have no memory of hot weather. However, it must have been a happy time because I have no unhappy memories which often, together with the real dramas of life, seem to be the ones which linger longest. In later years we would meet with the Howards when they came to Sydney and I knew them as warm and loving people.

Chapter 11

Dick Craymer was a city kid on a farm.

Around early May 1942 my father Max Craymer sent me (about 9½), my brothers Graham (5½) and Alan (3), together with our mother Aileen Craymer, to a farm at Mogongong near Grenfell NSW. Although we lived away from the coast at Eastwood we can conjecture that Dad may have had some 'inside' information. Having returned from WWI, Dad worked as an accountant with the Sydney City Council and after the outbreak of WWII, he was rostered to work at nights as a 'roof spotter' stationed on the roof of the Town Hall to look out for enemy aircraft. He was also an Air Raid Warden for the street in which we lived in Eastwood. During the first war Dad had met Eric Pfeiffer and they became firm friends, so it was arranged that Dad would take us to Eric's farm, Glenairlie, near Grenfell. At the time, the closest railway siding to the farm was Mogongong, between Cowra and Grenfell. The railway has not operated for many years and my brother Alan and I could find no sign of the old siding.

Glenairlie was a mixed farm with wheat, sheep and pigs. Although it was autumn and winter, I remember some quite hot days. One of the pleasures was learning to ride a children's bike and just about riding the wheels off it around the compound near the homestead! The two horses were called 'Six Bob' and 'Rose', but I cannot remember the names of the dogs – I was frightened of dogs at the time! My brother Graham remembers climbing a haystack, going to Church on a dray with all the other kids and seeing a Maxwell truck on the farm, no doubt because his second name is Maxwell. Alan, being only three years old at the time, has only vague memories. Eric Pfeiffer and his wife Connie, a typical farmer's wife, were welcoming hosts and their five children, particularly the older girls, were friendly enough towards these strange kids from the city. Their daughter, Stella reminded me that my mother's health broke down while we were at the farm so Dad came up again around August and brought us all home. But as we were away from the city in May of 1942 we missed all the fun of the Japanese midget submarine attack on Sydney Harbour!

Joan Craymer remarked on the lasting friendships that came from times of stress, when true feelings were shown in actions and worried parents were reassured that their children were being cared for

Letter of sympathy from Max Craymer to Stella (nee Pfeiffer) on death of her mother 13 May, 1974:

> *Often and often we talk with gratitude of your Mum and Dad in taking Aileen and the boys in 1942. It was a great relief to me to know that whatever happened to Sydney – and perhaps to me – they at least were as far away from trouble as was humanly possible, and in very good hands. For a few months at that time it seemed that a big city on the coast was no place for a mother and her three young children. Going further back I still live again in memory the happy times we had (Max and Eric) in our army days with your Dad's dry sense of humour and his infectious chuckle especially when the joke was on him. He was a really fine man to have as a friend.*

People who immigrated often kept in touch and helped each other. Single child families were unusual in the 1940s. Large families visited relatives during the Depression and for holidays. Grandma's, aunts and uncles' places were favourite destinations.

Chapter 12
Mum Slept Through the 'All Clear'

There was general panic ... with poor Dad having sent his family away for safety, now here they were, in the middle of a Japanese invasion! Mum was a bit more sanguine about it all, and I remember her saying that I was no safer in my bed so I might as well be up watching the fireworks.

– Anthony Euwer

A Carefree War

Mosman NSW was considered a target area because of its proximity to the Harbour. Shirley Hazzard, the novelist was evacuated from there to Penrith and spoke gloomily to friends about having to help with the cows.

Mosman Day Nursery School teachers, (shelled in May 1942), searched for a safe haven for their preschoolers and found premises at Ariah Par and Burradoo, south of Sydney. Joan Fry, a teacher at Tahmoor recounts challenges of evacuation in Leone Huntsman's book *Sydney Day Nurseries 1905-2005*: 'We didn't have a radio, didn't have a telephone …We had to walk about a mile to a pub phone every night. You had to boil the copper and bathe the children. You had someone dressing and undressing the children and someone in the other room telling stories. And the sanitary man ceased coming. So we thought 'here goes, we have to do it'. So we tied a handkerchief round our mouths and dug a hole miles away and we got the giggles carrying the can …. Sixteen went down with measles in one fell swoop. We rang the doctor in Picton. There was no petrol. He couldn't come out. We tried to get a nurse. We couldn't get a nurse. We sent 10 children home. Two of the children developed pneumonia, so for three days, we (the teachers) sat on a mattress in front of the fire eating oranges because the children kept crying and waking up. And I'll never forget the smell of measles, ever ...'

Leone has a story herself:

Mum evacuated with the three of us to the town of Young at the urging of her brother-in-law, the state member for Young. There we shared a house with relatives from the other side of the family. With three or four adults, and seven children under ten, it would have been a very crowded house at times. I don't know how long we stayed there, but it must have been a rather miserable time for Mum. Dad was an air raid warden so he needed to sleep at his workplace, the Commonwealth Bank in the City; he had to be around to manage things in the event of an air raid. He came to stay with us when he could, and I can remember racing downhill to jump into his arms as he walked up the long hill from the station. We all got sick in Young, with impetigo (contagious in a houseful of children) and measles (I seem to have had complications, and was sick in bed for a long time after the spots disappeared). Eventually it must have been decided that the Japanese threat had receded and we returned to Sydney.

An evacuee joke from the *Molong Express* entitled 'Underdone':

Two girl evacuees were billeted on a farm. One day, they accompanied the farmer's wife on her rounds of hen houses and came back with a basketful of brown eggs. The next day they went with her again and collected more eggs. On the third day they were allowed to go alone. When they came back, one of the girls said, Here they are. We left two because they aren't done yet. They are still white.

Ron Goodhew was just three years old when the war broke out in Europe, so remembers little of its early part:

Since I was nine by the time world peace was restored, there are plenty of memories of that time still racing through my head. It was not a pleasant time, even though we were never actually invaded in any serious way. Of course there was the submarine shelling of Newcastle from waters off our coast when the Japanese ventured this far south. And there were air attacks on Darwin, but that seemed so far away it could have been another country to our north.

But the effects of war still came to us. Food and fuel rationing was one. Our cars and trucks sprouted inflatable bags to hold gas to run our vehicles when petrol was so very short in supply. Then there were other means, like modifying engines to run on kerosene, so you would start up on petrol and after a mile or so of warm-up the driver would turn a tap or two to switch to kero. Vehicles didn't like it much and their performance was poor, but we got there just the same.

Although the risk of air raids was slight, all our windows needed to be blacked out so our lights would not give away our presence to attackers at night. Air raid shelters were even built by some citizens in their backyards, but I can't ever remember one at our place.

A Carefree War

My father was always bitter because he was prevented from joining his brothers and sister by enlisting in the service of his country. The patriotic fervour was much stronger at that time than might exist today. Dad was considered a primary producer, of food in particular, so was one that needed to stay home for the national benefit. But that was not any consolation to him, so he joined the Voluntary Defence Force (VDC). This was similar to what we currently call the Reservists. But, because we were at war, the VDC trained more regularly. In fact, most weekends would be taken up with such activities in various parts of the district.

Then my mother was not to sit on her hands either. She became an aircraft spotter. Now you could imagine, there were very few (in fact there were none!) enemy aircraft in our skies. But these spotters had to learn the shapes and distinguishing features of all types of enemy fighting planes so they could record their movement in case they invaded us.

Mum and Dad took their war service very seriously, so much so they decided to send me away for quite a while during one part of the war, I suppose they felt they could do it better without a young child to get in the way. Well, that is the reason that I have been told, but it has always puzzled me somewhat.

You see, my aunt (my mother's younger sister) had recently married and moved to a little home of her own, so offered to take me in. Auntie was miles (240 km) or so away. My maternal grandparents also lived in the town, as my grandfather, Bertram Teasdale, was night officer at Lawson railway station. We invariably spent time at their place over the Christmas holiday, so the location was not unfamiliar to me, even at that early age.

Well, I can't be precise with the date when I moved from Morisset to Lawson, but I believe I was about seven. I certainly spent my first year at school at Morisset Primary, but started there aged six, straight into first class, bypassing Kindergarten. It was awkward for Mum to get me to school and I would have started

Chapter 12

mid-year in any case, so they thought I could wait for first class instead. It didn't seem to adversely affect my schooling. I always enjoyed school and did reasonably well at it, without being in the genius league.

I remember something of my stay in the Blue Mountains. Joyce and John Leggatt had a very small home in a street behind the shops at Lawson. John was a baker in his father's bakery, so worked very early hours. I think my aunt also served in the baker's shop part-time. Being of school age I was sent to Lawson Primary, which was so easy to get to (by comparison with the 1.5 miles walk at Morisset) because it was at the end of our short street, just a couple of hundred metres from 'home'.

I cannot be sure of dates when I was brought home, but it was before the war had ended, because I can clearly remember the joyous celebrations of peace in the streets of Morisset town. I figure that it was about 18 months that I had spent at Lawson school and I finished out my primary learning at Morisset.

Lance Roper:
I was born on 4 July, 1932 and lived in Lewisham, Sydney. I had an older brother and sister. My father was a stock inspector and my mother a teacher. In 1942, there was much panic and many people were getting away from impending invasion. All they wanted to do was get away. As a boy of ten, I just did what I was told. The plan was that the eldest boy, who had won a scholarship would board at Riverview, Margot, my sister, would become a boarder at St Vincent's, Potts Point, and I would be sent to Katoomba, my mother already had a teaching position at Katoomba and I would go to De La Salle, Katoomba. We would board there while my father kept everything going and worked at Homebush, sometimes being on guard, visiting us when he could.

Katoomba used to be a romantic, rather charming place and it changed in the 1940s. The boarding house we were in was full of evacuees. We talked and played Chinese Checkers, and all got on well. The St Vincent boarders stayed at Mount St Marys. My mother taught at the local public school, which was a Methodist hall or church with a curtain down the middle.

I still love to visit Katoomba - it brings back happy memories of the year we spent there.

As children sat swinging their legs at the kitchen table, eating Vegemite sandwiches and Aeroplane jelly, they would be told they were going and that was that. They thought they were going on holiday, often to Grandma's or an aunt and uncle's place, where they had been before for holidays or during the Depression. Fortunately, most children did not realise what was at stake. Everywhere in war zones, mothers calmed their children, making light of the situation.

War is a time of severe dislocation, pressure, sadness, elation and definitely of change. The men who went overseas were often young, naive and full of adventure, with no idea of what awaited them, lucky to escape unscathed and often traumatised. Men who were unfit or in protected occupations now had additional responsibilities to support other civilians. Everyone was under pressure. People in voluntary organisations worked harder than ever. Women found themselves with careers and responsibilities they had not dreamed of. Children who were evacuated were also changed. The little ones, who can hardly remember anything, were safe and happy in the company of their relatives and friends, with their brothers and sisters and sometimes mothers, so life went by in a golden dream of sweet sleep, happy games and laughter. Children who went away by themselves were more likely to experience feelings of dread that would stay with them throughout their lives.

Jean Macleay gives us a child's view of the war:

> I really hadn't thought that there was anything interesting about my early childhood, but being reminded that it was somewhat different from the way things were both pre and post war I have been remembering some of the things that affected me. I think like most children I assumed this was just the way things were. The actual war was some strange distant happening that really

didn't have anything to do with me. Moving because of the danger of living near the coast appears to be not uncommon. We moved from Burwood to Eastwood. These days that doesn't make a lot of sense but then, in 1940, Eastwood was the back of beyond, a rural area of dairy farms, chook farms and we had a brick pit behind our house.

My aunt lived at Bondi and saw and heard the fuss when the Jap subs came into the harbour and Dad felt that shells could possibly reach Burwood being an inner western suburb. Trenches were all the go and something of a status symbol as to how fancy they were. I remember our neighbour over the road had a state of the art job with roof of which he was very proud. Dad wouldn't have any of that. He said that if he was going to die as a result of bombing then he would do it comfy in his bed ... besides it would mess up his very productive vegie garden and fruit trees. Trenches were also dug at Eastwood Primary School, cut quite deeply into the Eastwood clay. At first we were lined up and marched into them carrying a little bag that mum had to make. I can remember there was a peg to bite on (what for?!) and I think something like a gas mask.

We had a summer storm soon after they were dug and the trenches filled with water and didn't dry out until after the end of the war. Dad was over 40 and a solicitor at the Registrar General's Department so he was never called up but he did join the VDC. I can remember his coming home after all night out on training expeditions just in time to don his suit and go to work. Apparently they used to stomp around the paddocks where Macquarie Shopping Centre now stands in full uniform and waving guns. Dad's gun stood in our hall beside the telephone table!. One of the farmers came out one night and told them they were mad as he had rabbit traps set in his paddocks and they were lucky no one had stepped into one. Really children my age had no idea what a war really was, only that the Japs might get us. The only inconvenience I can remember experiencing was that I couldn't have enough butter on my toast as a result of which I have too much to this day. I can remember mum having ration books and complaining bitterly about not have enough cigarettes and also complaining that I was growing too tall and took too much material (it must have also been rationed) to make me a dress.

Glebe residents felt exposed by their location with, 164 factories employing 4,496 people. Lola Wooley's father was employed there in the war:

I was eight in 1940. We lived in Glebe, where Dad was the worker s manager for D Hardy and Sons, Timber Mills. At that time there was a lot of industry there - a sugar refinery, oil. My dad decided to send my mum, granny and myself to Katoomba to safety. I had an older brother and sister who had left home by then. My mum had been born in Katoomba and her house was still there. We lived in another little house, (often freezing), for about two years. We couldn't go to the school, we went to the Town Hall, down from the Carrington Hotel. It was so cold, no heating, we kept our jackets, mittens and 'pixie' hoods on all the time.

At the school, they dug trenches. Dad visited us when he could. I got toothache. Dad said to mum to bring me back down to Glebe where my dentist was. Would you believe it, it was the day the subs came into the Harbour! There was a special room at the Mills in case of invasion, with supplies in and we spent the time there.

Peter Andrews Coles has good memories of his childhood wartime experiences:

I went with my sister and grandmother to their uncle and aunt's farm, Garthowen. I, as a child, was not aware of the gravity of the time or the community concerns. The thing that stood out in my mind and has remained with me was the change in our settled life at Penrith and the excitement of the adventure to the country. The evacuation for us was in no way a distressing experience as we were fortunate to be moving to be with part of our loving, extended family.

Chapter 12

Martin Dobson was only small, but can think back to the early forties:
I was a little lad and we lived in Middle Street, Waverley. My
father worked at the gasworks. We went to the Blue Mountains for
about seven months, Katoomba, I think. I remember going in to
where they were vaccinating the kids and they were all screaming.
Next door was the Christian Brother's College, and they had a
huge basement in their building. When the Japanese subs came
into our Harbour, all the neighbours in our block took shelter in
the basement for three or four hours.

Meryl (Johnstone) Hanford had an adventurous time when she left Sydney:
When I was four or five and my brother, Geoff, seven or eight, my
mother announced we were 'going on holiday' and my father drove
us to a wool property called 'Willowmouth' near Coonabarabran,
which belonged to distant relatives. I remember I had my tonsils
out two days before we went and everything seemed very hasty.
My father returned to Sydney and my mother and I slept in one
room and my brother alone in another room. My mother was
worried about Geoff and got up early to check on him. His bed
was empty. She went downstairs and he was sitting up with the
shearers having breakfast!

It was reported in the *Sydney Morning Herald,* 19 February, 1942, thirty-
one children and six mothers, evacuees from Paddington, arrived at
Griffith and Narrandera, followed by a kindergarten teacher the next day.
They all knew each other. The children slept on straw pallets, the mothers
on beds. The mothers bought the food and kitchen work was rotated.

Mary Moss:
In 1942, my mother took my sister and me from Russel Lea to the
Riverina. There were AA guns at Rodd Point near us. We had slit
trenches in the back garden and stores of tins of food. My mother
went outside one night in the blackout to look at the searchlights
and an air warden came and told her she should be inside. She
told him she would decide when to go inside. The adults were
all frightened, but my mother told us exactly why we were going,

and I was excited. A widowed aunt of my mother's had two rice farms started on a soldier's settlement from World War 1. We went up by train. The names on the stations were blocked out.

We went to a little school with one teacher and seventeen children, from kindergarten to sixth class. We walked to school, a long way, in often 100 degree heat, and back home again. There was one man in charge - the others were all away fighting, - so everyone lent a hand. I sewed up the chaff bags with a big needle. My mother stayed with us. My father had electrical burns before the war. He had been knocked back for service in World War 1, because he had a heart murmur, (but he lived until he was 84!).

Bruce Whitefield only has happy memories:
I was born January 1934, in Sydney, and by 1941-42 Dad was in the army and somehow Mum and I were evacuated to Condobolin. I don't recall much of it except that it was a good time - we all (even us kids) learned how to weave camouflage nets and our Mums seemed to enjoy it all. It was a happy time for us kids.

Norman Owen left Rozelle for Griffiths:
Our family lived at Rozelle and my dad was a truck driver for Dunlops. When the Japanese bombed Darwin, Mum took me and my sister, Pat up to Griffiths by train to an orchard owned by an uncle. It was fun there and the food was good. We went to school about two miles away. I doubled my sister on my pushbike. We helped pick, sort and stack the fruit. It was like a holiday. We stayed a few months and we didn't see Dad until we went back home.

Joan (Elson) Bourke was close to the shelling at Bronte.
I was born in 1930 at Bronte. I was the youngest of five - all the others were older - from six to 18. Dad, from England, was a bricklayer, too old to join up. He was a warden and patrolled the streets to see no lights were shining. When the Japanese invasion looked imminent, we knew about them because we were close to Clovelly, so the shells were about a kilometre away. One of my sisters had a young baby. Father decided we had to get away.

Chapter 12

Mum didn't want to go. My brother's children aged four and six went to a tiny place called Derriwong, outside Condobolin, to my sister-in-law's auntie. In the end, my sister and her baby, my mum and myself went to Windellama - about 25 miles out of Condobolin. Dad always got the *Herald*, and he saw this ad:

The Sydney Morning Herald, Monday, 12 January, 1942

To Let Half House to mother and children, Mrs F H Boreham, Buburba, Windellama, BOOKER BAY - Cottage.

It was a long trip up to these people and we stayed there with Mr and Mrs Boreham and their son and daughter for about four months, from January 1942. It was a farm with chooks and cows. The one-room school had a red dirt playground with a map of Australia on it. It was two and a half miles across the fields to get to it. The mailman came three times a week by truck. There was no general store, you had to go to Condobolin for supplies, just a Post Office and a school. My sister's husband made the long trip up by train and then rode his bicycle the 25 miles every Friday night. One night he didn't arrive and we were all worried. He had come off his bike in the road and was found next day with a fractured skull. He eventually joined up, which he should not have done after his head injuries and came back after the war a changed man. After my brother-in-law's bike accident, my sister didn't care what dad said and we went back to Sydney. After about two weeks, the Japanese submarines came into the Harbour. Dad said I had to go to the same place as my sister-in-law at Derriwong. My eldest brother took me. There was another one-roomed school. The teacher lodged in the same house with us. Our hostess, a great-aunt was very strict and had ideas about children which were 'old school'. As the youngest, I was a bit spoilt and didn't like being told to 'eat everything up' and things like that. I have good memories of Derriwong: rabbit trapping, milking, fruit picking, getting the eggs - all a big adventure really. I missed mum, but I was never frightened. I made friends with the local kids and stayed friends with some of them all these years.

A Carefree War

Judy Suttor , (who settled happily in Armidale) was evacuated there:
At the end of 1941, when my parents decided to send me to
Armidale I was just five years old. I know that they were sad to
see me go, but that year, the first of my conscious memory, was
a great experience. At that stage I was an only child, my father
was an Oral Surgeon and my mother a professional pianist. We
lived in a Federation cottage in Double Bay and my childhood
was happy and uncomplicated. The journey by steam train from
Central Station in Sydney to Armidale took about 12 hours and
I travelled with my aunt and her small daughter and a family
friend, actress Queenie Ashton's older daughter and son.

We arrived to move in on my grandmother, known as Huttie who
lived in one half of a rented premises in Brown Street, with my
great aunt and great grandmother living in the other half. In the
yard of the 19th century house was a detached brick building,
perhaps once the kitchen or laundry, (or both), known as
Mulberry Cottage for the huge mulberry tree beside it. Here my
aunt and the other three children slept, while I had a bedroom in
my grandmother's side of the house. My grandmother and great
aunt were both music teachers and my great aunt had the care of
eighty-three year old Grandma Wharton, who was in the early
stages of dementia.

Grandma Wharton spent most of the day knitting khaki socks
for soldiers and my great aunt spent most of the night undoing
her work, re-knitting it and adding some. I started school in
Kindergarten at Armidale Demonstration School, which was only
a block away and I walked there with the two older children. We
all came home at lunchtime for a hot meal and scampered back
to be in time for afternoon classes. I also had a 'built-in friend',
the daughter of a Double Bay friend and neighbour who also
came to Armidale and was living with friends of my grandmother.
Particularly in winter we children often rugged up and went to
the picture theatre to the Saturday matinee and everybody always
walked to the Presbyterian Church each Sunday.

Chapter 12

We walked everywhere, but one lady sometimes picked me up in her little car and took me to visit the children at the Orphanage. I found this huge institution cold and forbidding and was somewhat overcome by the numbers of children, too many to single out anyone as an individual friend. A neighbour took over a vacant block nearby and grew enormous quantities of vegetables so that we and other families were always supplied with fresh food and we used to walk down to the butcher shop on the corner where the floor was covered with sawdust and there was a flyscreen with a sliding window between you and the friendly butcher.

In my mother's memoirs she writes, 'We had missed her (me) so much .. . the only way to be able to suffer her absence had been to fill every moment with work. My time was well filled with working for the Dental Comforts Fund and playing at Educational concerts for the troops. Most of these concerts were at Army camps such as Ingleburn and at hospitals, the former at night and the latter during the day. Army cars with chauffeurs were provided but often I would be the last of the artists to be delivered home, sometimes well after midnight.'

She also acknowledged her mother's 'magnificent War Effort' in looking after four children between three and nine years of age. Obviously adaptable and surrounded by caring family and friends and with a minimal knowledge of the hideous happenings of the war, except that my four uncles were serving overseas, I had a happy time as an evacuee, with the added bonus result of an enduring love of New England.

RDB (Wal) Whalley, remembers Armidale, where he too eventually settled:
The dark days of World War II in 1941 found my mother, my three sisters and me living at Mona Vale, north of Sydney, while my father was in Malaya with the AIF 8th Division. At this time, an invasion of Australia by the Japanese seemed imminent. The beaches of the Warringah Peninsular north of Sydney, including Mona Vale, were being heavily fortified, in the belief that they formed an ideal site for an invading force to land. As the youngest,

A Carefree War

I was eight years old at the time and was very interested in all the military activities.

My mother decided to move the family inland so that we would not be in the front line if an invasion did occur. I understand that she chose Armidale because she knew Mr Gordon Hutchinson, Estate Agent, and so she wrote to him asking if there were any possibility of obtaining rental accommodation for herself and her four children. She had a Bachelor of Science degree with Honours in Botany from Sydney University and I also understand that she put her qualifications at the end of her letter. The outcome was that we did move to Armidale and took up residence at 200 Jessie Street. The house (since demolished) was large and rambling, on the southern side of the railway line and overlooked the present roundabout on the southern side of the railway bridge. The slope below the house to the New England Highway, then, as now, was covered with Cootamundra wattle trees. My mother taught biology at PLC (then at Brown Street) and also assisted teaching Botany at the then University College at Booloominbah.

The Fletcher family lived next door to us with Neville (then about 12 and later to become Professor of Physics at University of New England) and his younger brother, Ian. Ian was a year above me at the Armidale Demonstration School (now Armidale City Public School) and he and I spent many hours collecting insects and preserving them pinned to cork in collecting boxes.

We made our own amusements in those days before the advent of electronic entertainment. The Fletchers had some old Edison cylindrical wax gramophone records that could no longer be played. Neville wanted to see if he could make a gramophone record and so we melted several cylinders in my mother's best saucepan on the stove to produce a flat disc. Neville then drilled a hole in the centre of the disc, and placed it on the turntable of our gramophone (powered by a spring and with a steel needle). He then guided the needle in a more or less spiral path towards the centre of the disc while the rest of us yelled as loudly as we could down the speaker of the gramophone. When he replayed our 'record', the needle faithfully followed the spiral and we could faintly hear our voices coming through the speaker.

My mother was concerned about two major diseases because this was before the days of immunisation and antibiotics. One was polio and the other was pneumonia. There was no defence against the first except cleanliness, and her defence against the second was to ensure that our respiratory systems were as robust as possible. This meant that we all slept on a veranda through the Armidale winters and we all escaped both of these diseases. I certainly was used to the cold because I can distinctly remember running down to the bridge across the small creek near the present Armidale Cemetery in the early morning in winter, in shorts and with bare feet, and running my finger along the bridge railing and watching the long frost crystals fall over my finger.

One morning in February 1942, I woke up and found my mother in tears in the kitchen. We had not heard from my father since the invasion of Malaya had commenced and she had just heard on the morning radio news that Singapore had fallen, and of course, had no idea of what had happened to Dad. We heard nothing for some weeks and then suddenly a telegram from him was delivered from Townsville, Queensland. It turned out that before hostilities commenced, he had become very ill because he had absorbed large quantities of chromium from the khaki dyes used in the uniforms of the day. This had given him severe dermatitis before hostilities commenced and he had been sent to hospital in Singapore. He and fellow patients were evacuated by ship some 72 hours before the surrender on the 15th February, 1942 and after some weeks of dodging enemy warships, made it to Townsville. He later joined us in Armidale and during the rest of the year, he alternated between time here and periods in the military hospital in Croydon, Sydney. The whole family returned to Sydney about the end of 1942. The dermatitis gradually declined over the next 20 years or so.

When he was in Armidale, my father had to keep himself active to keep his mind off the continual itch of his dermatitis. Weekends were often spent in long walks along Dumaresq Creek to Commissioners Waters for picnics, catching yabbies in the water holes under the willows. My father had been a boarder at TAS and so he knew of many other picnic spots in the district as well. My mother would invite boys boarding at St. John's Hostel (now part of NEGS) to spend a Saturday with us to give them a bit of home life. We kept up with some of these young men for many years.

The site of the present water reservoir for South Armidale off Garibaldi Street was an abandoned gravel quarry at the time, and had magnificent blackberries growing up the sides. We found some old sheets of roofing iron and would use them to flatten the thorny bushes so we could reach the most luscious berries during blackberry time. We also had a Mulberry tree and so raised many silk worms and laboriously wound the fine silk on to pieces of cardboard after the larvae had pupated. I had some of these for many years but they have all disappeared by now. Other amusements were putting two crossed pins on the railway line at the Butler Street railway crossing and then searching for them after the Glenn Innes mail had passed. If we were lucky, we could find the two crossed pins welded into a miniature pair of scissors by the pressure of the heavy locomotive wheels.

Those two years or so that I spent in Armidale made a big impression on me, and I have many happy memories of our time here.

Alan Ecob has a romantic memory of a little evacuee:
Her name was Frances Heinz and in 1942-43 she lived with her aunt in Kurnell and attended our one-room public school. She was the same age as I (11 to 12) and had been sent south by her Queensland parents because they feared Japanese invasion. She was a typical girl of that age and that time with regular features, lightly tanned skin, brown hair and eyes and average build. I would have liked for us to have become friends, because in our eight-pupil school, only two others were near my age, and neither

were friends. But it was not to be. Frances avoided friendship, perhaps because her aunt dissuaded her. So she made no friends and was seldom seen outside of their house. She was better at school than I. In every exam she was always a couple of marks ahead of me. Dad niggled at me to do better, but my impression was that if I did, Frances would simply lift her game. Still, the challenge ended in mid 1943 when her parents took her back to live with them in Queensland.

Les Reedman was in a target area in Newcastle:
Our family lived opposite an army base in Adamstown, Newcastle. We built an air raid shelter. In 1941, we moved to Belmont because BHP was a target area, as was Nine Mile Beach, from Redhead to Blacksmith, near Swansea, (actually six miles long, but a good possible landing place). We returned to Adamstown in 1942, when I was about seven, and I remember looking through the window as the Japs bombed BHP.

Anthony Euwer:
When my parents thought the Japs might attack, Mum and my sister and I were evacuated from Newcastle to Denman. Mum had discovered a farm in Denman which would take paying guests, and we all got in the train and headed west. Dad had to stay behind in Newcastle to work in a protected job at the BHP. I was intrigued by our new life, and found the farm to be a fascinating place, and I immediately became a farmer, aged seven. I can still smell the farmhouse kitchen, the kerosene lamps, and the cow-bails. I still have some of the scars I collected from a ferret, and a cart wheel.

I feel quite sorry for the poor farmer. He was stuck with a family he did not want, a two-year-old girl, a boy who asked never-ending questions and wanted to be included in everything, and their very disapproving parent. Lately we have found that visitors are like fish. They go off after three days. How he managed to put up with us for the six months we spent with them is beyond my imagination.

Until she had to give it up when she got married, Mum had been a primary school teacher. Her grammar was flawless, her knowledge quite wide, and she was very scornful of her 'inferiors'. I seem to have inherited some of this unlovely trait. The farmer and his family were good solid salt-of-the-earth people, but Mum disapproved of their speech, their swearing, and just about everything else they did. We ate with them, and their table manners included things like tossing the loaf of bread from father at one end of the long kitchen table to son at the other end. Mum was suitably horrified. Looking back on this, I expect they were exaggerating their coarseness and crudities, specially for Mum's benefit. I know that in the same situation, I certainly would.

I managed to con myself into everything that was going on at the farm. I milked cows, separated cream, churned butter, shovelled dung, and made a general nuisance of myself. They let me drive the horse and cart sometimes, but I never did get the hang of cracking a whip properly.

Once when I was riding in the cart, I was hanging on to the side of the cart, and as we went through a bump, the wheel wobbled over and ground a bit of my finger off.

We went rabbiting quite a lot. Rabbiting presented interesting challenges. Putting a chicken-wire trap in EVERY hole in the rabbit warren was really important, because when you finally put the ferret down a hole, the rabbits would race out all the other holes and into the traps. Any hidden hole without a trap in it was a great escape route, and you could also lose your ferret! Getting the ferret out of his sugar bag and into a hole should have been simple enough, but I managed to get his head out of a small hole in the sugar bag, and he expressed his gratitude by biting the same finger recently ground down by the cart wheel. Hence the scars, which have remained to this day! I learnt to kill and skin rabbits, and nail the skins up on the wall of the cowshed to dry.

There was no school nearby, and several children in need, so the next door farmer, about a mile away, built a small shed out of corrugated iron, for a schoolhouse, which soon became known as the Tin Bitsa. His daughter became the 'teacher' and while I expect she did her best, she was not qualified, just well meaning … There were about eight or ten of us, of different ages, so getting through to all of us would have been no mean feat. I was learning more on the farm!

The Tin Bitsa Schoolhouse was considered too far away for a small boy to walk, so Dad turned up to visit, bringing a beautifully done-up red push-bike! It was explained that this was a great privilege, and I was to take great care of it. The route to school was partly across the paddocks, and partly along the road. The route was alive with a particularly virulent form of prickle, known as goat-heads, or three cornered jacks. They are seed pods designed to be spread by sticking into anything passing, and they punctured many tyres. They are tetrahedron shape, so no matter which way they fall, there is always a sharp spike sticking UP. I set up a wooden vee shaped cotton reel to run on each tyre, so it would pull the spikes out as fast as they went in. This worked really well.

After school the other boys with bikes raced down the hill to the gate, and I followed. Not noticing that they all rode close to the gatepost, I sailed through the middle. There was a big pothole in the middle … My new bike stopped dead in the hole, but I sailed straight on, flying right across the road, and landing in the blackberries on the other side …

They say that wisdom comes from experience, and as most experience is loud, painful and expensive, I should have absorbed huge amounts of wisdom by now … I must have learnt something, because even now, seventy years later, when I see a long line of traffic, and an empty lane, I say to myself, 'What do they know that I don't?'

While I was at the farm, the kids who had not been evacuated were still at Mayfield West, being introduced to their Times Tables and Arithmetic. I was happily milking and rabbiting, and learning very little of any use in the Tin Bitsa. When I got back, I was way behind in everything I suppose, but losing that introduction to tables, and arithmetic was disastrous. I have never really caught up!

I loved Geometry and Algebra, because they involve logical thinking, but if it involves anything to do with Calculus, get someone else! I have really resented the dud deal I got with Maths, as it has affected a lot of life choices. I blame the horrible Maths teacher mostly. He coached the top football team, and spent parts of every lesson up the back of the room He once hit the Mayor's son behind the ear where he had a boil. John Norris got straight up and decked him! When witnesses were called for, no-one had seen anything … I survived by picturing him in his bath, or on the toilet …and reciting James Shirley's poem, *The glories of our blood and state.*

Mum hatched a plan to secretly make a surprise visit to Dad in Newcastle for a few days in June 1942 and we got on the train. This was undoubtedly also a respite visit for Mum from the indignities of the farmhouse. Poor Dad! He was certainly surprised! He had his bike in a million parts all over the Lounge Room! Mum expressed significant displeasure and disappointment … She was really good at that … While we were there, I got the flu, and we stayed on longer, as Mum quite rightly decided it was easier to nurse me in our own home than up at the farm. Any excuse not to go back!

So we were still there in our house in Mayfield West, for the night of 8 June, 1942, when the Japs attacked! There was general panic in our house for a while, with poor Dad having sent his family away for safety, now here they were, in the middle of a Japanese invasion! Mum was a bit more sanguine about it all, and I remember her saying that I was no safer in my bed so I might as well be up watching the fireworks … We watched a few hits down the hill in Waratah…

Chapter 12

Dad helped me build a trolley which was the name given then to a billy cart made with ball-races for wheels. Very fast! Very noisy! Very low. I roared across the Buruda Street intersection to the butcher once, straight through under a semi-trailer! All my mates had a trolley, and we used to race down the footpath, much to the annoyance of one crotchety old hag opposite who we delighted in tormenting by riding past her house. I used it to go to the butcher to get a 'Pound of shin beef, chopped up very finely please!' I had no idea we were poor … Mum's 'grey stew' was magnificent! Mutton chops were the base, and goodness knows what else, but we loved it!

Our landlady over the back fence, had the only phone in the area and so I ran a lot of messages.

After a year or so, my mates got their own bikes, and my popularity declined … More experience. Their bikes were shiny black, and my beautiful red bike suddenly became black, much to Dad's displeasure. It's the last time I remember succumbing to peer group pressure! I was about ten by then. I have been studiously doing my own thing ever since. To hell with other people's opinion. My mother used to say, 'My face I don't mind it, for I am behind it. It's those out the front get the shock!'

Children had their own world of billycarts, playing with the dog, football, comics and cowboys and Indians. 'Can I go out?' was the often asked question, and rainy days were not good days. They played war games. An *Australian Women's Weekly* reporter, December 1941, was told 'Taking Cover'? was 'Practising - you're out in the street, you throw yourself down on the ground like this, and raise your head and chest on your elbows like this and keep your mouth open, then the bomb goes bang! and you're alright, see?'

Arnold Meaker, who lived in Newcastle, thinks his father evacuated them well before any attacks.

I was born at Mayfield in 1932. The family lived with Granma Meaker in Ingall Street while Dad built our future home at 16 William Street Mayfield. When I was nine or ten years old, Dad worked as a builder at the big storage sheds on Lea Wharf (in the Honeysuckle area). Whether he was advised to evacuate us kids or maybe it was an inclination of some sort of attack we were moved to a house in Lord Street, Dungog. This was before the eventual attack on Newcastle. We resided in Dungog for about two years. My eldest brother, Trevor was too old to attend public school and it was considered too expensive for him to go to high school in Maitland. We, my other two brothers and two sisters spent a fair bit of time going to the Army Training Rifle range over the hill from the showground, or we'd wait for the trains going north with the soldiers on board, who were handed meat pies as the trains never stopped but rolled slowly through the station. Great were the tasty meat pies that sometimes dropped. This I remember quite vividly, just as much as the pinching of the juicy oranges hanging over the fence (I was dobbed in to the headmaster by a classmate). The house we lived in must have been owned by a very keen gardener, with all those strawberries in the back yard. I assure you that none of those strawberries got really ripe. In 1953 I got married to a girl from Wallsend, Gloria Dickson, (we are still married), and it turned out her uncle Abe lived in Dungog and she and her family went to live with them in 1942. She is three years younger than I and guess what, she also lived in Lord Street and was at the same school, no! I didn't know her then.

Cecily Atton was evacuated from Eastwood to Narrabri with her sister. We lived at Eastwood. There were a lot of Italian market gardeners and they were interned. Dad was a paymaster on Garden Island. My sister and I were evacuated to my mother's sister and her husband, Auntie Sadie and Uncle Dick, who had no children, so that we could go to a convent school at Narrabri. We had no idea of what might happen, we were very naive. If I had heard anything bad, I would not have known what it was. To get to Narrabri, fourteen miles away, we had to catch a little train called Lulu. We waited at the 440 mile post, watching for the puff of smoke in the distance. Permission was given for Lulu to stop and pick us up. We got into the guard's van to Turrawan and then we got out and into a carriage. Coming home, we'd catch the Sydney train.

The most noteworthy of our trips on Lulu, (at the time I thought so anyway), was the day the Governor, Baron Wakehurst visited Narrabri, and how I remember the opening lines of the welcoming speech given to him: 'To His Excellency, The Right Honourable John de Vere 2nd Baron Wakehurst, Rightful Order of St. Michael and St. George, Governor of New South Wales. We, the children of Narrabri, welcome you, and your noble wife Lady Wakehurst, to our town and school'. Although we were not VIPs, the Vice Regal Carriage, connected to Lulu, had to stop allowing my sister and me to get on, so I suppose for that moment we were VIPs ! Our aunt and uncle were wonderful we'd holidayed with them since we were little. We had beautiful country food from the property. They made their own butter and we collected the eggs. Turrawan 6 was the telephone number. We phoned home every week.

Children were also evacuated from inland suburbs, as Winsome Shepherd relates:

> A couple of cousins from Artarmon were sent to Mudgee, to one of the aunts on a property. My grandmother and grandfather were there.

Port Kembla, as a safe harbour with good roads just south of Sydney, was a likely target. At night enemy signals and flares could be seen.

Marie (Jilroy) Hellmund:

> I was at Keiraville, an inner suburb of Wollongong, with my family, which being on the coast and near Port Kembla, was considered a dangerous place. Submarines belonging to the Imperial Japanese Navy were very active off the east coast of Australia. At least five 'I Class' submarines patrolled the waters off NSW. Between 1940 and 1944 twenty-two ships struck mines or were torpedoed, resulting in the loss of 244 lives. In June 1942, the MV *Echunga* and MV *Orestes* came into contact with submarines directly off

Port Kembla but evaded them. A month later the *George S Livanos* and the MV *Coast Farmer* were both sunk near Jervis Bay.

When the Japanese submarines came into Sydney Harbour, in late May and early June 1942, and made a series of attacks on Sydney as well as Newcastle, my parents felt they had to do something about us children.

I knew about the war because there were anti-tank pyramids in Heritage Park. We watched the Breakwater Battery being built in 1939 as the headquarters for the defence measures and a coastal defence battery against enemy shipping and submarines. There were up to 120 troops (both men and women) from the Army, Royal Australian Artillery and the Volunteer Defence Corps.

There were two 6 inch Mk Xl guns near the southern breakwater at Port Kembla. In 1942, they built the Drummond battery at Mount St Thomas and Illowra battery, also known as Hill 60 Battery, as a counter bombardment battery. There were also two BL 9.2 inch Mk X guns and searchlights.

I was about eight or nine and in the middle of the family when we clambered into the back of a truck, with my mother's sister, her two daughters and two of her sons, and a friend and her two daughters. We went to Mittagong and stayed with one of mum's in-laws at the back of Frensham School. I don't remember what was said, and I didn't have a feeling of danger, we all just climbed into the back of the truck with all the stuff. Dad worked at the steel works, a protected industry, and had to stay. The time passed pleasantly for us ten: we went to the local school and the movies and had each other for company'.

Barry Hishion describes a short-lived evacuation to Glen Innes from Wollongong:

At the outbreak of WWII in 1939, my wife Marie's parents, Hugh and Eileen Costello (nee McClifty), were living in Wollongong where Hugh was a Manual Arts teacher at the Wollongong Technical College; both were Glen Innes people.

Chapter 12

At that time the Australian Iron and Steel Pty Ltd at Port Kembla (Est 1928), then developing production, soon gained the Federal Government's attention. To protect the works and the shipping traffic that served it, one six inch gun was installed on a hill in the suburb of Mangerton, overlooking the family home at Coniston. It was named Fort Drummond and as time would show it never fired a shot in anger. Another that was installed on Hill 60 overlooking Port Kembla was named the Illowra Battery. With Japan's entry into the war in December 1941, the Steelworks was considered a prime target to attack, being cause for local people to become jittery. As Japanese activity in the Pacific increased, Hugh decided to send Eileen and the children to Glen Innes for safe keeping. Taking Marie with her older brother John, they were driven to Sydney by Dr Finlayson the family doctor. He happened to be going to Sydney early that morning and with train timetables restricted, this was very convenient. They left Central Station on the Glen Innes Mail for a 12 hour trip as Marie recalls, with the train being packed with soldiers. As some took to sleeping on the luggage racks this saw their cases being squeezed between the seats, making for uncomfortable seating. Their retreat to Glen was to be of short duration, for not long after Hugh was taken ill with appendicitis, requiring Eileen to return to Wollongong with the children. During their short stay Eileen said that she saw more of the war effort in Glen Innes then than she did in Wollongong or Port Kembla. Daily she witnessed lines of trucks carrying loads of military equipment passing through the town manned by soldiers, heading north to Brisbane.

Lynton Bradford, listening to one of my talks, realised after all these years that he had been evacuated!

I didn't realise it at the time, but no doubt I was sent to Gerringong after the shelling at Bondi and the submarine attack in Sydney Harbour. Actually I was away from Sydney until after the end of the war, although I was only at Gerringong for about two years until I was due to go to high school. Then I was sent to All

Saints Boarding School at Bathurst for about two years, then on to Griffith High School until the war ended. I commenced work at Griffith for about year, but the firm closed, so I returned to Sydney and started an apprenticeship.

He wrote *The Fig Tree*, a piece inspired by his stay in Gerringong. He has fond memories:

> At night it was pitch dark, no electric lights, no neighbours nearby, just the faint, distant sounds of waves crashing endlessly on the rocky shore and on starry nights, the black shadow of a huge fig tree blotted out half the sky. These were among my savoured memories of this special place. It had no running water, sewerage, telephone, transport of any kind a young boy would expect in the early 1940s. Why then do I retain such fond memories of this home? Letters were simply addressed as 'Boat Harbour Gerrigong, NSW'. The nearest houses were almost a kilometre away.

Boat Harbour had no modern amenities, no electricity, running water, sewerage, telephone, transport of any kind, or any of the conveniences a young boy would expect in the early 1940s.

Lynton:

> I lived with my great aunt Grace Watkins, after whom my mother was named. Charlton, (the name was rarely used), was her family home, built and added to by her father, Frederick, as his family of 13 grew. It had never been the subject of any council approvals. In fact, there were no councils in the area when this home was started in the mid-1800s. To have a bath, we opted for the kitchen, where there was a fuel stove to warm the room, and a round galvanised iron tub, requiring many trips to the spring, some 100 metres away, to fill to a depth of about 50mm. Two baths a week were considered ample, considering the effort required. It was a hard, but rewarding life at Boat Harbour. The chores included collecting wood for the big fireplaces, fowls to feed, eggs to collect: walking up to the town for milk and supplies. A large mantel radio used a car battery,

which had to be taken to the local garage, about two kilometres away, for charging. It was my job to drag it uphill in my billy cart, with many stops on the way, then collecting it the next day. Consequently, the radio was only used to listen to the news once or twice a week. The lounge room was heavily curtained and so dark you could not see to read, even in broad daylight. There was an organ with pump pedals, which was the only luxury in the house. The beds had mattresses of duck feathers, so deep you sank almost from view, a huge mosquito net draped from the steel and brass canopy over the bedhead. Each room had its china wash basin and water jug and of course a potty. The dunny pan needed emptying about once a month. A deep hole was dug in the vegetable garden and to avoid digging it up again, there was a plan of rotation. Of course the dunny paper was cut up newspapers or magazines. With luck, you could read up on stories by assembling the cut sections while contemplating. However, more often than not, essential parts of the stories were not to be found. The original dunny was very fragile after 90 years and was tied to a large peppercorn tree. Unfortunately, the peppercorn blew down in a gale, taking the dunny with it, so a new one was built. I had a fox terrier called Tinker and we went everywhere together, exploring the rocks and seashore also rabbit hunting, but never caught anything as I recall. The only remaining landmark is a great Moreton Bay Fig tree planted by my grandfather in the mid - 1800s and no doubt nourished throughout its life by the buried 'treasure' in the vegetable garden.

Alan Wilkinson recalls two evacuees that his grandparents, staunch Methodists housed on their fruit farm, probably through church connection:

Geoff Northcott and Ian Newton are seen here happily helped on the rubber drive. A neighbouring farmer had a pile of rubber tyres which had been flung down an old well. They were pulled out for the war effort. Somebody offered Mr Yeoman's rubber bed sheet and there were jokes going around because he was incontinent.

A Carefree War

Mrs Shirley Killeen's family said the submarines in the Harbour were enough for them to pack up and leave:

Just after the Japanese entered the Harbour, five of us went up to our cousins at Cowra, where a new baby was born. We must have come by train but I don't remember it. Mum must have been upset to leave Dad, but she didn't show it. Dad was in the police force. They told him that he wouldn't be able to look after us if anything happened. I was seven when we left home. We all slept on the veranda. It was cold. We had mosquito coils smoking away because we were near a river. The first day at the new school I was sent up to the Principal's Office because I moved after the bell went. I didn't know that you had to stand still. We went down a lane to school and we used to rub our hands on the leaves of the peppercorn tree in case we got the cane. We were well fed. There was a lovely apricot tree in the garden. The railway line ran along the back of the property - which is still there. Albert's father worked on the railways and he used to throw coal down as he went past. There was an air raid shelter in the back garden with a corrugated iron roof. We used it as a slide. We went swimming in the Lachlan River. My elder sister yelled out there was a shark once, but it was a floating tyre. I think we were away about a year - it's hard to remember. We had a carefree war.

Chapter 13
Going to Grandmas

*I didn't like it much at grandmas. She got me up at 5 am.
I had to feed the chooks and every now and then she'd cut
the head off one and it would always be my favourite.*

– Richard Featherstone-Haugh

A Carefree War

Associate Professor Bev Kingston:

Can I draw your attention to: *An Imperial Affair*, Monash University Publishing 2013. There on p. 79 John Rickard describes how his grandmother and mother, sharing a flat in Manly while his father was on active service in London in 1941, decided to move because of the fear of invasion. So they moved to a house in Gordon that was vacant because its owners 'were taking flight to the Blue Mountains'. Not long after the battle of Midway the owners of the house in Gordon decided it was safe to return to Sydney, so Rickard's mother and grandmother were house hunting again. (p.81)

John Taylor remembers Manly Beach with barbed wire:

We went up to the Blue Mountains to escape the Japanese. Mum took us six kids to a holiday house my grandfather had had at Mount Victoria, a Queenslander style home with six bedrooms, and we were there when the Japanese submarines came into the Harbour in May 1942. Our youngest was aged four and Mary was taking the Leaving Certificate. For 12 months, we went by train to St Bernard's College (now Katoomba High School), and back to Manly for the holidays. Dad stayed at work at City Mutual and when we were in the mountains, caught The Fish as the train was called then, up to stay with us on Friday night, going back on Monday morning.

Some grandmothers went away. Judy Suttor said the Blue Mountains were a popular retreat:

My grandmother and her sister both had houses in the Eastern Suburbs and they went to the Blue Mountains - that's what people of their class did.

Bill Deeley lived at Dulwich Hill with his family:

I remember the submarine nets that let the ferries through. When the Japanese came into Sydney Harbour, my parents had gone out and I was with my grandmother. She was the youngest of her family, born when her father was sixty years old. I was about four and a half. We got under the table with a mattress on the top. After that we were sent by train to my grandmother's sister's house at Coolah. It seemed huge to us. I don't know how much acreage she had. Outside the house there was a shed and a water tank. I remember running around in bare feet and getting into trouble. I remember grasshopper plagues - you couldn't walk without crunching on grasshoppers. The lady of the house had chooks and a turkey. When Christmas came, she killed the turkey and cooked it but we wouldn't eat it and cried because it was our friend. Her husband lived there but her children were 20 years older than us. He was a foreman in a box factory, a protected industry.

Some grandmothers were taken with their families or grandchildren being evacuated. Peter Coles (Andrews):

Judith, my sister, my grandmother, Grace Williams-Neville and I were evacuated in 1942 to Garthowen to the farm of Frank and Hilda Fragar. They are my uncle and aunt, Hilda being my mother's sister. I have fond memories of 'Garthowen', of Auntie Hilda, Uncle Frank, Lynne and Nessie. In 1942, with the war situation for Australia rather desperate, the Japanese Army advancing in New Guinea, midget submarines entering Sydney Harbour and destroying ships and the prospects of an invasion, mother, in her usual way, made plans to evacuate Grandma, herself, Judith and me out of what she saw as harm's way. She found a small cottage somewhere where we could go, saved enough petrol or petrol coupons, and her plan was in place should an invasion take place, In the meantime, Grandma Neville, Judith and I went to stay with the Fragar family at Garthowen.

For me it was a joyous experience on the farm, even though lessons had to be completed each morning under Auntie Hilda's tutorage, but once complete, I was free to join the men. This may mean riding my bike to collect the mail, helping Lynne crotch sheep, witness the killing of a sheep for meat, helping Uncle Frank cut chaff and muster sheep, rabbiting with Lynne - just so many things for a boy to do.

Auntie Hilda conducted correspondence Sunday School and of course I had to be part of this. However, she made it fun with lessons down by the river or panning for gold in the creek and was always able to weave God's message into the experience. I could go on for a long time as so many things remain deep in my memory of the time with the Fragar family that the time was not one of worry about the war but a unique time to remember and cherish for a life time. The evacuation for us was in no way a distressing experience as we were fortunate to be moving to be with part of our loving, extended family.

Some grandparents stayed at home, visiting their evacuee grandchildren - taking turns if there were two available. Children were often used to staying with them and after a good scrub down with Lifebuoy soap, clean underwear and a hankie, packed their bags going off happily, blissfully unaware of the reason for going. For worried parents, it was a blessing to picture their children on the rug in front of someone else's fire, the mantel clock ticking away in the peaceful room, playing 'Snakes and Ladders', while they waited for tea. Knowing who would be caring for their children was important. To achieve this, some went two hours drive away, some went interstate, and distance was not an issue, as one woman said:

We went from Sydney to Shepparton, Victoria, because that's where our grandparents were.

Richard Featherstone-Haugh:

I was in Camperdown children's hospital aged six and a half, having my tonsils and adenoids out and the nurses put some of our beds out on the veranda, because there were so many children. We were eating our jelly and ice cream when there was a terrible noise and all the lights everywhere around and in the hospital went out. Searchlights moved about the sky and sirens went. It was something in the Harbour. I think we could see across there because there were very few tall buildings. The nurses hurried around taking all the kids into a basement where mattresses were laid out. Kids were crying for their mums and I was frightened. I heard someone say, 'The Japs are here'. The nurses gave us lemonade for a treat and tried to quieten everyone down. The nurses wanted to get back to their families but the transport had stopped. Rumours were flying, like 'The Japs have landed at Maroubra'. There was a feeling of panic. The next day my mother came and took me home to Eastlakes. The day after, my little sister and I were put on a train to Orange, with a lot more children and Red Cross nurses looking after us all. The children got off at various stops. My father said he could have bought a house in Vaucluse, Rose Bay or Double Bay for £250. We were going to Grandma's place and she met the train. I was up there for two years but my little sister cried all the time for her mother and she came up and took her back. I didn't like it much at Grandma's. She got me up at 5 am. I had to feed the chooks and every now and then she'd cut the head off one and it would always be my favourite. Dad was up in New Guinea. When he was discharged, he came up and took me home. We were held up near the Victoria Barracks and there was a big brawl going on between American servicemen and Australians, with girls sitting on the kerb crying their eyes out.

Grandma could be a 'staging post' whilst one or two of the parents tried to find a place to rent. Bill Willett was eight when they moved away from the bombing:

My family had to move away from Townsville in 1941/2. My father was away with the RAAF and the Japanese dropped a couple of bombs close to Townsville. My father rang my mother from wherever he was and told her to 'go as soon as you can'. We walked out of home with just clothes in suitcases. I was the youngest and had three sisters. I went to my grandmother's farm at Zillmere, with one sister. She had a chicken farm and sold eggs in Brisbane. There was a horse there. The others went to relatives at Highgate Hill, Brisbane. After a while, mother found a rented house at Eagle Junction and we were together once again.

Dad told us that we should evacuate as soon as possible because the Japanese were getting too close and he wanted us out of there. None of us can remember whether they had actually dropped a bomb (bombs), but I can remember being told that they had dropped them. My eldest sister was a young nurse at the Townsville general hospital and it was thought that she should stay as she may be needed. My sister said if the family had a car, it had to be left with a full tank of petrol and nothing other than some clothing was allowed on the train. My sister stayed at the house at West End (which was almost next to Garbutt Aerodrome) and she was looked after by a fellow nurse. I never saw her for a few years, until she arrived in Brisbane. One of my sisters and I stayed at my Grandmother's farm and the others were at Maleny, just north of Brisbane. When my mother arranged to rent a house, the family got together again and the job of finding furniture, beds and necessities began - all second-hand stuff from auction rooms. The departure from Townsville was 1941 approximately but that is not exact as far as my sisters are concerned. It was a long time ago and for me, I was just a carefree 8 year old boy and did not know what was happening anyway.

John Martin and his sister, Margaret Helen (now Wiseman) went to their grandma's place near the South Australian border:

My parents must have really thought the Japanese were coming. They sent my sister Margaret, four years older and me to my mother's mother at Casterton near the South Australia border. They had a farm on the Glenelg River banks, in fact there were three farms all belonging to family members. I was six. I was bewildered but Auntie Dot in the farm next to Grandma's had ten children, so there was always someone to play with. We stayed for the best part of a year, the happiest time of my life. I still have a wind up gramophone, I like old things. They had a phone, but I only remember it being used once or twice while we were there - I think my parents wrote letters. I don't think they ever rang. My uncle used to yell into it because it was high up on the wall. None of the three farms had electricity or cars and tank water. I don't remember seeing money, they traded rabbits, and ate pigeon pie and vegetables. They had cows for cream and milk. Auntie Dot never left the kitchen. She just went from the bedroom to the kitchen and stayed there all day. On their veranda was the biggest bath I've ever seen, and all the kids got in it and the water was so dirty that my sister and I walked on past and got into the river, luckily not far to go! Dad had a butcher's shop in Cliftonville, out of Melbourne, so food was never a problem. Mum was the cashier. We had a delivery boy for the butcher's shop, Martin, and he would ride around Collingwood with his basket laden with parcels. Sometimes I'd get a ride on top of the parcels.

Father was only a few minutes away from the shop. He decided to build a little weekender at Lilydale with his father. He bought a Rickenbacker car. The company was established by Eddie Rickenbacker, America's leading fighter ace during World War 1. He flew a SPAD S.XIII, a French biplane fighter developed by Société Pour L'Aviation et ses Dérivés (SPAD), one of the most capable fighters of the war, with orders for around 10,000 cancelled at the armistice. He put his WWI 94th Fighter Squadron emblem depicting a top hat inside a ring, on both the front and the back of the car, and there was gas producer at the back of the car.

Dad got conscripted. Mum made him a cut lunch. Off he went, they found he was in an essential industry and back he came. Mum was a Red Cross driver and dad was an air raid warden. His place was the centre where everybody met up with their masks and gear. There were trenches everywhere. At Casterton, there were four men in the Middle East. They came back and were sent on the Kokoda Trail. One got killed. Mum and Dad would come and visit and they would be loaded up with clothes - the family was always short of clothes and they'd hand them out. Coming back the 240 kms, they'd be loaded up with rabbits and vegetables. My mother had a good way of cooking rabbits with bacon round them.

Some families could not afford evacuation. A Mrs Gale, with eight children, said her mother, on a farm in Gundagai, had offered to take the children for the duration. She told an *Australian Women's Weekly* reporter she would willingly send them, but the eldest boy would pay full fare, and the others half fare, and her husband's wage would not allow for it. She would wait for the government to do something. Meanwhile she had plenty to do and not enough time to worry.

Laeonie David's father-in-law made the decision to evacuate.

My husband's father sent his pregnant wife and five children to
Young in 1942 when the Japanese were threatening to bomb
Sydney Harbour and they remained there for about 12 months.
My husband was born there and the older children went to the
local catholic primary school. Regular visits by my father-in-law
were made by train, as petrol rationing forbade any unnecessary
travelling and both grandmothers took turns to stay with the
family whilst they were there.

Some grandmothers cared for other children. Jenny Hanson:

My grandmother had a friend in Sydney, with a daughter who was
about twelve, the same age as my father in the war years. This girl
came up from Sydney and lived with my grandmother for about
two years. She was an only child, but her parents were terrified of
the Japanese coming and felt she was safe there.

Families travelling by car needed food with them. The *Wollongong
Argus*, August 1942, published advice on what to take for a carload of
five for two days: Any bread, cake, scones etc in the pantry at the time
should be taken, two large tins of fish or meat, two large tins of fruit,
one small packet of biscuits, one small jar of peanut butter, one packet
of Kraft cheese, half a pound of wholemeal biscuits, a jar of Vegemite,
Marmite or Bovril, half a pound of tea, coffee or cocoa, one small tin
of milk, one pound of sugar and a small quantity of salt. In addition,
dates, nuts and raisins, chocolate, glucose and barley sugar could be
packed - don't forget the billy can!

In working families, the youngest would be sent away. Alan Fletcher
remembers his family splitting up.

I was living near Tamarama in Sydney in the early 40s and was
voluntarily evacuated, for the 1942 calendar year to Yenda, in
the Murrumbidgee Irrigation Area near Griffith. I was born
November 1930, so had just turned 11. My elder brother, born
June 1928 was also evacuated but the eldest brother, born in
1925 and other cousins did not move out of Sydney. My family
situation at the time was that my father had died in 1937, my

sister, born 1915 was working in Melbourne and my mother was caring alone for her three sons. There were other aunts and uncles and cousins living around Tamarama.

Empty houses from deceased estates were not unusual. Bill Geoghlin and his family used such a house:

I am one of a family of thirteen. I remember adult males with cameras had to pretty careful where they took photos, due to security fears. The house we went to was I think, part of my deceased grandparents estate and had sat unused and there were very few buyers (if any) and it was not uncommon for houses to remain empty for years ... No sane person would holiday in my country town. It is probably difficult for younger people today to understand the utter simplicity of life in those times. We weren't brainwashed by TV, or newspaper commercials. In fact as a boy the only newspapers I read were behind the dunny (toilet) door. We had no grand thoughts of careers or Universities, (which only admitted people of means). We went to School but weren't educated. School for the average boy was a place you went to and couldn't wait to get out of.

At some stage in the war seven of us (six girls) and me were sent back to a country town a long way from Sydney where there was a family house unoccupied and where my father had a business which was classed as essential industry. My brother was in the RAAF. The oldest of the girls was about 15 or 16 years. She had virtual control of the household apart from Dad's occasional interference. It really wasn't a bad experience overall even without Mum in Sydney. The older girls were subject to decisions by the Manpower authorities in some cases and in one case were sent to work at a factory which was two hours from our Sydney home. We were able to continue our schooling at the town's Catholic school and I don't feel we suffered any disadvantage from this.

For some reason we were returned to Sydney but following reports of Japanese planes overflying Sydney and the midget submarine raid, back we went to the bush to the same situation as before, except another sister was in charge of us. I can only remember the good bits. But it was hot and dusty and there was some resentment by some town kids against the 'blow-ins'. We always seemed to have plenty to eat. People would kill a sheep, the baker still ran his shop, and fruit and vegies were always available. There was food rationing and my father couldn't get enough petrol to run his car so we used a horse and sulky if we had to travel anywhere. Plenty of milk, DIY butter, eggs laid on, and mostly it was home cooking and whatever we couldn't get we simply did without it without any concern.

When the war situation improved we came back to Sydney. Rationing carried on for some time after the end of the war and I recall going to the grocer with ration tickets in hand. In terms of running a household, at least for food, it was a lot easier in the country (from my perspective). I spent a lot of time going out to various farms with my father where he used a steam traction engine to provide a huge belt drive to a chaffcutter or hay presser. He employed a handyman cum cook to feed his work team and a mobile cookhouse went with us when we moved on to other farms. Needless to say, I spent a fair amount of time with the cook. He was actually able to provide plenty of roasted meats, gravies and damper washed down with hot billy tea for the men who refused to drink it on payday because they 'saved their thirst'. Actually they were paid in the pub on Saturdays. There was not a lot (or even any) entertainment - there was a 'picture show' in town, very occasional Sunday football at the grounds, at which lovely pies were served, but we often sat on the veranda with some of the neighbours in the hopefully cooler twilight armed with the *Boomerang Songbook* and sang for hours.

Australian evacuees made the best of it, with grandma there to give warmth, comfort and advice. If you were lucky, grandpa would be there too.

Chapter 14
No More Flowers – Western Australia

At one point virtually all the women and children in Geraldton were evacuated. We thought the Japanese would come down the west coast, as we had training fields for them to land. We thought Perth would be blown off the map.

– Stan Gratte.

A Carefree War

Secession was a recurring theme in Western Australia from 1829, but in 1942, they were caught up in the same war related problems. The author, Randolph Stow, born in Geraldton, was evacuated for a short time to family properties in the hinterland in 1942. This shaped his novel *The Merry-go-Round in the Sea* about a Geraldton family. In the book six year old Rob goes inland to Sandalwood Homestead, and there is talk of fleeing to Bogoda Station, Mount Magnet. The little boy doesn't understand. 'The war was a curse, a mystery, an enchantment. Because of the war there were no more paper flowers. That was how he first knew the curse had fallen. Once there had been little paper seeds that he had dropped into a bowl of water, and slowly they had opened out and become flowers floating in the water. The flowers had come from Japan. Now there was a war, and there would never be paper flowers again'. Stan Gratte was in a hive of activity. The whole district became one big army camp, with tents everywhere in the bush, trucks, jeeps and motorbikes with troops:

At one point virtually all the women and children in Geraldton were evacuated. We thought the Japanese would come down the west coast, as we had training fields for them to land. We thought Perth would be blown off the map. A lot of troops moved in to fortify the area. Bridges all around were stacked with gelignite and the authorities blew large sections out of our long jetty. My dad worked in the plotting room. He spotted a little plane that came round about 30 miles north. The RAAF rang up when it went over the town. They thought they might bomb us that night and told everyone to 'get out of town'. We had a lot of service families. My wife went to Allenooka, but people went to the little mining towns around where they knew someone. We took the dog. While we were away a lot more servicemen moved into the area. I was 12 years old and it was a great adventure for me. I'm quite sure my parents were scared, but I wasn't. We were encouraged to do plane spotting. Wherever you went there were illustrated charts and Kellogg's put out a book of planes. We hung up model planes on lengths of string so we could look up at them. Hot, dry Wiluna, on the edge of the western desert, was supposed to be of interest to the Japanese for its mining activity, especially arsenic, which they needed for gas bombs.

Chapter 14

From his book *A Boy and the War* Stan says:

We were warned at school to steer clear of Army installations and we thought about those bayonets the guards had on their rifles. This warning eventually wore off and we got quite cheeky as all boys do. I know we climbed over the two metre high sandbag walls around the American set-up and got into the gun pits. There were boxes of 30-calibre ammunition in steel clip belts, in boxes, in the walls. We'd peel a yard of ammo off and skedaddle over the wall. We'd pull some to bits to see how they worked. Chuck some in a fire to hear the bang or swap some with your mates for Perspex or whatever you could get. I guess that sort of thing goes on wherever there are armies. And I expect other boys pinched gunpowder off Napoleon's soldiers.

George Cusins lived on the Perth Road:

Our whole family went to an old farmhouse we rented in the middle of wheat fields. We drove into Geraldton for supplies. I wasn't scared. I was excited with all the army personnel and equipment in the town.

Harold McCashney's parents were concerned that Perth would be bombed:

I was evacuated from Bassendean, a metropolitan suburb of Perth to Cadoux, (named after Donald Cadoux, an early settler who died in World War 1), about 180 kilometres northeast of Perth. My sister went with me to my father's sister and her husband. They didn't have any children. I can't really remember much - it was a 15 hour train journey on a freight train that stopped a lot - I was seven. We were very well treated. They had a farm - 1,000 acres or so - with good food. My dad was a wagon builder for the WAGR, a government job. My mum stayed with the two other kids, one older, one younger. There wasn't a phone at the farm or in the village. We had letters from home.

Patricia Wood's father was interned in Singapore:

There were quite a few people - women and children - who were evacuated from Singapore in January 1942 in troop ships that had dropped off British troops to defend Singapore. Many people didn't believe they would be staying long because of the defence of Singapore. That didn't succeed of course. In our case, my mother decided to leave the ship at Fremantle because it was the closest place to Malaya for when it would be OK to turn around and go back to our home there.

As it turned out, by 1943 we obviously weren't going back, so my mother was able to buy a house near the beach quite cheaply. Houses in the coastal areas near Fremantle were sold and families had moved inland, so I suppose we benefitted from the displacement experienced by local children who were evacuated from the coast at that time. It's an odd world! We have published a book that is made up of letters from my mother to her English family and the diary that my father wrote in internment in Singapore. It's called *If This Should be Farewell.*

Lindsay Carter thought he was going on holiday:

I can recall being sent to a farm in Pinjelly south of Perth with my older brother. I was not aware of the situation at the time, probably thought it was a holiday. I remember very little about it. I was born in 1936, my brother three years older. He remembered a lot more, including the name of the farmers but has sadly passed away. The only events I can remember about the farm was being sent in search of hen eggs in the sheds under farm machinery etc. and finding some of them rotten, riding around the farm on a horse and cart early in the morning laying rabbit bait, very exciting, and being scared to hell by an wedge-tailed eagle hovering above me. Years later in my late fifties I had a weird dream recalling the incident vividly. The dream told me that the eagle had not meant to scare me but was sent to protect me. May be I was a bit traumatised by the whole episode.

Chief Evacuation Officer F Huelin said: Big families who have to be billeted have given billeting officers a headache. One family of mother and father and ten children will have to be evacuated. 'We shall endeavour not to split families, but if we have to they will be put as close as possible to each other,' Mr Huelin explained.

Chapter 14

People of the romantic city of Broome believed they were out of range of the Japanese fighters, did not fear invasion and then overnight became a staging post for allied aircraft. Timor was invaded, providing a Japanese air base at Koepang within striking distance of north Western Australia.

Dutch, American, British and Australian naval and army forces had fought the Japanese around the Indonesian Archipelago, throughout February 1942, but the Japanese war machine advanced relentlessly, and many military planes arrived in Broome, carrying Dutch refugees. The attack on Broome was heralded by a Japanese Kawanishi flying boat, 50 metres over the town. Six flying boats had landed each with over 30 Dutch refugees. There were limited facilities for refuelling or for ferrying passengers to shore, so they waited in the military planes.

On the airfield, Dutch military pilot Gus Winckel, had stopped to refuel his Lockheed Lodestar, after getting his passengers to safety. Guessing his plane could be a target, he removed one of the mounted machine guns and waited. Nine Zero fighter planes armed with machine guns and 20 millimetre cannons and one navigational plane approached from the north, sweeping around Gantheaume Point. People heard the *rat-tat-tat* of machine guns destroying the 15 flying boats. The Zeros turned their attention to Broome airfield. Six large planes on the Broome airfield and an American B-24 bomber were shot down shortly after takeoff with the loss of 19 lives. More than 20 children were amongst the almost 60 dead as people struggled for survival amongst the burning debris.

Mr Winckel said when visiting Broome for the 60th anniversary of the air raid, 'And luckily, one of them came very, very close to me and I gave him a long burst. And also, I shot him down. I wish I shot a few more down. I hit another one who had to dump in the sea.' The Broome incident fuelled invasion fears elsewhere.

The Australian government wanted their contribution to the war sufficiently recognised. Britain's Ministry of Information was consulted and they contacted Ealing Studios, who were enthusiastic about making a film. *The Overlanders* was the result in 1946, based on a true incident in 1942 when 100,000 cattle were driven 2,000 miles in the Northern Territory to escape the Japanese.

A Carefree War

The Overlanders is about evacuation and removing a food supply from the enemy, as drovers take a large herd 1,600 miles overland from Wyndham through the Northern Territory outback to Brisbane pastures. (The film makers had obviously not heard of the Brisbane Line). In the movie Dan McAlpine's character Chips Rafferty, empties his water tanks and sets fire to his homestead, watching the flames engulf his belongings, declaring grimly, 'The Japs will get nothing from me.'

John Nugent-Hayward's character Bill Parsons was also filled with the need to escape, fearing invasion, Parsons leaves his homestead in northern Australia with his wife and two daughters, Mary and Helen. They join up with Dan McAlpine's cattle drive south. The Japanese are never mentioned except for a scene where a plane comes over as they are droving and somebody asks, 'Is that a Jap?'

The movie was enormously successful at the box office in Australia and England; by February 1947 it was estimated 350,000 Australians had seen it, making it the most widely seen movie about Australia of all time. And a successful endeavour for the Australian government in war propaganda!

Chapter 15
Tasmanian Fears

*People just thought it was pretty sensible. A lot of people
got their kids out of town if they could.*

— Vera Fisher

A Carefree War

Tasmania has a recorded awareness of invaders since the coming of the Europeans. In their history as a colony, Tasmania was automatically at war with Britain's enemies and European rivals, such as France. Hobart Town was a vital supply stop for whalers and sealers, and a hub for the British ships. By 1942, 12 permanent defensive coastal batteries, (now boarded up), linked with tunnels had been built, starting with the use of convict labour in the nineteenth century.

During WWII, there were concerns Tasmania would be invaded by the Japanese, largely because of the state's zinc industry, vital to the war effort, but the official Australian stance was that Tasmania was an unlikely enemy target. Japanese advances made Tasmanians more keenly aware of their geographical isolation, in the uncertainty of the times, but as a small island off a large one, isolation became its strength. Fear of attack from the sea increased when German naval raiders *Pinguin* and *Atlantis* laid mines near the River Derwent mouth. After Tasmanian soldiers left for the North African campaign with the Australian 6th Division, Hobart was closed to shipping. Bass Strait was closed after a mine sank the British steamer *Cambridge* in 1940.

There was more alarm when HMAS *Sydney* was sunk off the Western Australian coast in 1941, as Tasmanian soldiers left for Malaya with the Australian 8th Division. A Japanese submarine-launched seaplane flew a spying mission over Hobart in March 1942. After this, two anti-aircraft guns were positioned on nearby hills, but the Japanese never returned to Tasmania.

Sir Robert Cosgrove, the wartime Premier and his government co-operated fully with the Commonwealth in putting Tasmania's economy on a wartime footing. Tasmania's economy was emerging from the Depression and ammunition factories in Launceston and Hobart, employing 1,600 workers were welcome. Wooden boats, prisms, textiles, metal works and other essential pieces of war equipment were also produced.

Evacuation plans for the civilian population were developed, and air raid precautions included building shelters, slit trenches and casualty stations, regular drills and 'brown outs', which intensified when the Japanese overran South East Asia and bombed northern Australia in early 1942, culminating in a trial blackout of the whole state in mid-year. Air Raid Precaution services were staffed by 14,000 voluntary workers and a Volunteer Defence Corps of 4000 men manned coastal and anti-aircraft defence positions. Civilians became used to the sound of artillery practice. There were at least four military aircraft crashes. *Civil Defence Regulations* 1941 on the front page of the *The Mercury* newspaper gave instructions on internal and external flying glass in the case of bombing. Trenches were dug around schools, for instance at the AG Ogilvie High School, where fathers were required to be at the school from 6 pm to 8 pm, Monday to Friday and 8 am to 12 noon Saturday, 'for the purpose of digging trenches for the protection of their children.' Tea was very kindly provided each evening for those coming directly from work.

Vera Fisher:

> We didn't have any evacuation plans at our house, but Gran and Grandpa at Fernhurst had an air raid shelter in the back yard. Grandpa was bedridden by this time, and he was on a banana lounge by day, ready to be wheeled down, so it had to be the width of the banana lounge to get him into the air raid shelter. Pam Davis, who lived at Pawtella, was attending Hobart High School, but her parents brought her home because she'd be safer up here. So she used to go to the Oatlands Area School in the Hobart High uniform. Then Fahan School took over the boarding house at Interlaken, and the accommodation house was totally Fahan students.

In 1942, the private girl's school Fahan was evacuated to Interlaken, on the Central Plateau for two terms, recalled as an idyllic time by students in the school yearbook. One of the teachers, Dr. Winifred Mary Curtis AM, PhD, DSc, FLS has been described as 'the botanist whose texts have defined Tasmanian flora.' She commuted every few weeks between the school and the university, to teach, with brief detours to National Park where her parents had rented a house. The journeys were adventurous because the wheelbase of the small family car was not wide enough to fit the ruts of the unmade roads.

The evacuees were lucky to have her because she was appointed University of Tasmania Senior Lecturer in Botany in 1951 and Reader in Botany in 1956, the most senior position held by a woman at the university at that time.

Chapter 16
I Want to Go

After about two and a half years, our parents came to get us, and there was a family row. Aunt Eileen could not have children and she said bitterly to my mother, 'You can always have some more' ... Aunt Eileen sadly referred to us two as 'my boys' for the rest of her life.

– Peter Daley

Chapter 16

Cassie Thornley:

My elderly cousin is 91, physically challenged but still bright. She says, 'We all knew the children were going to the country, people got together and organised it between themselves, and they went to relatives. An awful lot came down from up north.

As far as I know, there has not been an Australian film about the emotional turmoil caused by interfering with bonding between a mother and her children - an Ealing Productions film *The Divided Heart*, 1954, based on a true story, demonstrates clearly the unbearable emotional burden put on children and their mothers by separation caused by war. This story is based in Germany and Yugoslavia, but it also happened in Australia.

Peter Daley:

There were eventually six children in our family at Wollongong. At the beginning, my brother, who was older than me by less than a year and myself, born in 1939, were the only ones. We were brought up as twins. We were always close - I lived in his shadow. Dad was working at the steelworks and Wollongong and Port Kembla were fortified and considered dangerous. He was a trained fire officer and in a protected industry so he was well aware of the danger. Dad had a married sister, Eileen, married without children living at Cessnock and my brother and I were taken up to their house on a huge block, backing into the bush. We had our tonsils out just before going up and I remember eating junket and jelly to sooth the soreness.

My uncle went shooting most weekends - kangaroos, for the meat that he fed to his six hunting dogs. We were given one each for our own. I've kept dogs ever since. We pulled the blinds down at night and there were local searchlights.

Eileen's husband was a coal miner. He got killed in the pit when I was about eight. They were always good to us.

I remember my uncle getting bitten by a redback spider. The grownups used to talk about the 'Brisbane Line'. Everyone had chimneys and steel ovens and got their coal cheap and there was a special smoky odour right through the town'.

It's about 300 kms to Cessnock, no phone, so communication was only by mail. I don't remember if our parents wrote to us or visited us, because we were so small, but later in life I found out that after about two and a half years, our parents came to get us, and there was a family row. Aunt Eileen could not have children and she said bitterly to my mother, 'You can always have some more'. This is what Mum did - four more in fact. Aunt Eileen sadly referred to us two as 'my boys' for the rest of her life.

Margaret Elizabeth Joiner (nee Nancarrow) was homesick even though she was treated well:

I was 11 years old and lived at 430 Darling Street, Balmain. It was an old Victorian style cottage which was divided into two flats. A doctor and his niece lived in the other one. My aunt and grandmother (always known as 'Granny'), had a flat in Birchgrove Road opposite the Cockatoo Dock. My father enlisted on 11 June, 1940, and went to the Middle East and Tobruk. When he returned and the air raid sirens were being tested he would hit the decks at top speed. My mum came home from her work at DJ's department store one afternoon to find that her sister, Peg O'Donell and brother, Charles O'Donell had organised for Granny to go to stay with another sister who lived further inland at Carlton/Kogarah and for me to go to Leeton to stay with the Dunns, a family friend whom I had never met.

I was put on a train pretty much straight away – children did what they were told in those days so I didn't argue. I recall the train being very crowded (with civilians) and that it took forever because the train was often shunted onto side lines in order to let the troop trains through. I had just started at Fort Street Girls High School. I don't recall being scared, or any of my friends being sent away.

Chapter 16

The Dunns had a big house and they took in boarders – often girls who worked in the local bank. Quite often the girls were late home for tea because, in those days, they had to stay at the bank until they balanced their day's takings. The Dunns had three children: two girls and one boy. The older girl was about 18 and had gone to Sydney to do nursing and the other two were more my age. Mr Dunn worked for the council as a water bailiff – Leeton being a big irrigation area. He was in charge of turning the water on and off for the farmers. Often the farmers would give him peaches from their farms and I recall how good they were. It was in Leeton that I also had my first taste of mushrooms which I love to this day. Mr Dunn would collect them from the paddocks when he was out visiting the farmers. I recall getting mumps shortly after arriving at the Dunn's. They were very good to me – couldn't have been nicer - but I was so homesick that I started walking in my sleep and even got as far as the front lawn on one occasion. It was a night that the Dunns were entertaining the shire president and it was freezing so it caused a bit of a stir. I also recall getting chilblains for the first and only time whilst living in Leeton and recall placing my hands against the concrete walls to try and cool them down.

My parents wrote to me and I recall the beautiful script that my father had. I have happy memories of spending time by the Murrumbidgee River and being awed by its size and beauty. I would ride the bike that the Dunn kids had given me and taught me to master. My parents couldn't afford to buy me a bike so it was rather wonderful to learn that skill and to have the freedom that the bike afforded. At the Leeton school I was unable to continue my Latin studies as the Latin teacher at the Leeton school had joined the army. Each evening a troop train would stop at Leeton and I recall going very excitedly down to meet the train as it was usually full of American soldiers who would throw chewing gum to the kids. I stayed in Leeton until just after the Japanese entered Sydney Harbour. I think it was about six months. My father had returned by then too so it was decided that it would be best if I went home as I was still fretting. The return train trip was very similar to my original trip – crowded and slow. Sometime after my return home, I recall my father taking me to town one day to see the Japanese submarines – or what was left of them. I was fascinated and he bought me a piece of copper pipe (a piece of the submarine) as a memento which I thought was pretty special.

Judy Grieve, as President of the Armidale and District Historical Society, told of one of the few sad stories that surfaced after the war:

I received a letter from a lady who had been evacuated from Sydney to Armidale in 1942 during the war when she was around eight years of age. The letter was a request to know what school she would have attended. Based on the fact that she had been utterly unhappy, she had blotted out all memory of what was likely to have been a year of her life and she was trying to recall some of that experience. All she remembered her tearful father at Central Railway Station when she was bundled into a steam train carriage in a confusion of numerous other children and distraught parents on the railway platform. She moved into dormitory accommodation on arrival at her new home. In an effort to assist her I found that the CWA in Armidale was requested to find suitable accommodation in private homes for evacuated children and to report to a committee of Council, clergy and citizens. Newspaper reports from the schools in early 1942 indicated a massive increase in enrolments and that the girls' and boys' boarding schools were filled to capacity. I could not establish which school this lady may have attended, but did establish that a large home near a public primary school, leased by a teacher may have been a possibility and the names of both the home and the school gave her some glimmer of recognition. This lady's life was never the same, as by the time she returned her father had died and her mother had moved to a totally different locality and on talking with her on the telephone, she was still, in her seventies, profoundly sad.

Most children had a carefree war. John Martin says it was the happiest time of his life:

Chapter 16

We rode horses bareback at Casterton, at Grandma's place, about 40 miles from Mount Gambier. We used to yodel like Tex Morton, the yodelling boundary rider, go rabbiting with ferrets, and my cousin, who was about 7, had a .22 rifle. It wasn't until after my parents were both dead that I realised I had been evacuated. They never talked about it. I suppose once the war was finished, they threw up their hands and said, 'thank goodness' and that was the end of it.

Judy Thurgood's husband, Arthur, living at Haberfield has also recently realised why he went north. She says:

In talking with my husband, we've realised that the war may have been the reason his mother took him north to stay with relatives on dairy farms on the Richmond River near Lismore in 1942 (he was 5 years old in the June and started school in the district at Pelican Creek. His father was away in the Air Force at that time – he'd always assumed his mother just chose to stay with relatives.

However, in the 1940s, children would whisper to each other in their beds, listening to fragments of adult conversation, trying to make sense of it all. They must have seen their mothers weeping, sighing, staring out of the window for a long time, or into the fire, talking in low tones to their relatives and friends; children see everything, although they do not always understand. Some felt nervous but they didn't know why - they just felt the tension around them. The whole family was affected by things done far away and out of their control. 44Some people have remarked that it was difficult to know how other child evacuees felt at the time, because you did what you were told. You were not part of the decision making process. Mary Lark said she remembers her brother being sent away:

My brother, Bill Woodside, was sent from prep school in Toowoomba to Southport in 1940, when he was in Grade 6. His school was part of General McArthur's headquarters. We were on a farm at Guluguba and nobody talked much about the war, nothing was said about the war, so I don't know if he was happy or unhappy.

A Carefree War

It was very hard for mothers to let go of their children when it was impossible for them to go with them. On London stations, at the beginning of evacuation, relatives were allowed to say goodbye to children as they boarded the trains, but some snatched their children back at the last minute. Tearful mothers were eventually stopped by big black concertina gates at the end of platforms, hands stretching through, desperate for a last glimpse of their children, trying to be brave and pretend they were going on holiday.

Some people told me they weren't frightened, just unsettled. Anne Taylor went to Muswellbrook, but wanted to stay at home with her family at any price:

> In the Second World War, I went to Muswellbrook to stay with friends of my parents. I was twelve years old and not happy there, I couldn't settle. I insisted on coming home to Tamarama. I remember shells going over, but I wasn't frightened - even when woken up in the night and put on a mattress under a table in the hall with two young neighbouring boys.

In Australia, even teenagers, when they were used to a happy family life, could feel a bit lost, like Myfanwy Coleman.

> In 1942, I was living with my Aunt Kitty, at Manly. She took fright at the idea of a Japanese invasion and went to stay at Picton with a friend, taking her youngest daughter. Her older daughter went to stay with an aunt at Collaroy. I was 21 and going to work on the ferry. I felt abandoned. I had to find somewhere to stay.

Fay Sulman is keenly aware of the damage that war does. Her mother had a full and happy pre-war life. She worked at Nestlé's Chocolate Factory near Abbotsford, Sydney and went on several cruises. She married a handsome young man in uniform and had a baby daughter. And then the war came:

> My mother had a worrying nature and was very frightened by the events of the war. I was her only child and she was incredibly protective. I was born in 1940 in Newcastle, where my father was in the Army at Fort Scratchley. He joined up when I was

eight months old. He was in a Japanese POW camp. He came home when I was five, and it was never any good. My mother had worried about him so much when he was away, but his war experiences had ruined his life and I was frightened of him, especially when he was violent towards my mother. She always spoke about the war times but he never did. I don't think she ever confided in anyone. During the war, my mother moved around a bit, Newcastle to Abbotsford to be with her sister. When the Japanese came in, she was at Bondi. She was scared. Another sister said, 'The Japs aren't coming after *you,* Ruby!' Somehow she got a job at Burragorang, on a farm with an elderly couple, where she did domestic duties. She knew my father was in Changi. She said Mrs Jessup, the farmer's wife, was nice to her, but it must have been lonely, lying in bed by herself every night. My grandmother had three sons in WWI, and they all came home but they were damaged. It must have been terrible for her.

The suicide rate, which had risen in the Depression, dropped in the 1940s. It has been suggested that the fall in suicide and deaths among young men, typically the largest group in society to take their own lives, was largely due to the fall in road deaths because of petrol rationing, and the fact that they were overseas fighting. Explanations of suicide involve a complex interaction between psychiatric and sociological factors, and it is difficult to explain the drop in suicides at a time of social disruption, when marital stability is held up as a key factor in preventing suicidal behaviour. Looking at contemporary statistics, there is a surge in suicide, especially young males, when a suicide is profiled in the Press. But in the 1940s, all the stories were of death and destruction. There are many contradictions. Other reasons why can only be guessed at: there was more to fight for, with a clear goal, more unity and camaraderie perhaps, as Australians felt united against the enemy, patriotic and realising what a great country they had to fight for. This great threat gave a purpose to their lives.

Cassie Thornley, whose father was from Austria, remembers how displaced loyalty affected her sister.

Marie, whose father was Austrian, came home in tears from school (Katoomba High), a group of children had decided the family was 'German', and she was being ridiculed and ostracised.

Norman Longmate in his book *How We Lived Then*, page 75, tells the story of Robert, who aged three, had been sent to live with three elderly spinsters in Devon in the UK. 'He shocked his mother when she eventually visited him. At bedtime, he knelt down by his bedside and prayed,' Oh God, don't let this woman take me away; she says she's my mother but I want to stay here with my aunties.'

Chapter 17
Changing Lives

We didn't want to go, we were happy at the Mission, welcomed by the local community and I loved Penrith High School. I was the class captain and I wanted to be a doctor.

– Joyce Dukes

A Carefree War

Tomatoes! Hundreds and hundreds of tomatoes! Stan Gratte in Western Australia was a schoolboy volunteer to grow tomatoes to help feed the troops, Americans as well, and civilians. Aged twelve, he was allocated to a man he liked, a good gardener, who patiently explained how to grow things. Stan said that had a major effect on his life and he became a market gardener. Countless people's lives changed when they were evacuated, and some discovered a career path.

Grace Perry expressed her feelings of loss and abandonment as an evacuee in many poems, which her father, a journalist for *The Age* arranged to be published by the Consolidated Press. Entitled *Staring at the Stars,* her books sold for one shilling and she gained a following. Her books were sent in food parcels to Australian troops in the Pacific.

Grace was born in Toorak in 1927 and moved to Brisbane with her family when she was six. Aged thirteen, she moved with her family to Sydney, where her father, by now a published author, became Secretary to the Minister for Public Works in 1940. Grace was educated at St Gabriel's School, Waverley, near their home and in 1942, she was evacuated to Goulburn. When the imminent danger of invasion was over in Sydney, Grace returned, completed her Leaving Certificate and enrolled in Medicine at Sydney University.

As a married woman with three children and a career in medicine, she found it very difficult to find time to write, describing herself as 'a hologram' reflected in 'too many mirrors'. Somehow she managed to start writing again in 1961, and ran *Poetry Australia* for over twenty years, helping emergent poets like John Tranter and Les Murray. She published many volumes of poetry, received an Order of Australia in 1984 and the NSW Premier's Literary Award in 1985. Grace over-committed herself to her work, was refused funding, and crippled by arthritis could no longer walk to the post office. Feeling abandoned, she took her own life aged sixty. It is clear that her early experience as an evacuee had a huge influence on her work, with its echoes of loneliness, although she had a sense of humour, as can be seen in this excerpt from a poem in *Winter Diary from Berrima*:

> 'each night I face myself
> and fear to pass
> the hand-tooled tiger
> made of brass'.

Chapter 17

Sue Mackenzie recounts how her father changed careers:

I am the granddaughter of Robert Rolph, whose father started the *Launceston Examiner,* and I was living with my family at Manly in the 1940s. Manly Beach was covered in star posts and my father still has a big scar on his leg from falling on a star post (he wasn't supposed to be playing near the wire). In 1941, my father decided to evacuate my mother, sister, grandmother and me to Wallgrove Camp at Rooty Hill. My mother worked in the kitchen. Dad got a job with the horses. The American servicemen used to come up for RnR. They loved riding. Dad became so good with horses that he became a jackaroo.

Kerry Packer was a high profile and dynamic figure whose life was changed by being a child evacuee. His mother worked with the Red Cross and served as co-president of the *Australian Women's Weekly* Club for Servicewomen. During the war her adored only brother was killed and she herself was hospitalised with an undisclosed illness. It is said that his parents were inattentive and uncaring about him. Aged five, Kerry was sent to board at Cranbrook, near the family home. Not long after, following the midget submarine attacks on Sydney Harbour, he was sent to live with an aunt at Bowral in the Southern Highlands. While there, he contracted polio and pneumatic fever, spending nine months hospitalised in an iron lung before moving to Canberra for two years to recuperate. The polio left him with the left side of his face palsied. When he finally got to school, he was well behind in his studies and had a form of dyslexia, causing his father to refer to him as 'boofhead'. Broadcaster Phillip Adams, recalls: 'He never talked much about his mother except to point out that neither mum nor dad had much time to visit him when he was suffering from polio'. Out of this lonely, disrupted childhood, belittled by his father, who seemed to have favoured his older brother, grew a man desperate to prove himself. His first opportunity came in 1972 when he and Ita Buttrose launched *Cleo* magazine. His father never believed in the project so its instant success provided an enormous boost to Kerry's confidence. Eighteen months later, his father died and Kerry inherited the company, which became the base for his empire. His evacuation to his aunt's undoubtedly set his life on a changed course.

A Carefree War

A group in society whose lives changed course, and for the better were the estimated 25,000 'half-castes', as the term was then for children of Aboriginal and other race parents. There were about 11,000 of these children in New South Wales. They had been regarded as 'a problem' and were easily identified by authorities, because they lived mostly in camps or on mission stations. Those to be thought in danger from an invasion force, or occupying premises that were needed by the military, were sent to centres all over New South Wales and South Australia by army transport. The war was to change the life of many of those who came south, because they were a focus in the Press, and much to everyone's surprise, assimilated well with other children and achieved in sports and school subjects.

The profile of indigenous people generally improved as thousands helped in the war effort, as servicemen and labourers and were belatedly publicly congratulated and recognised for what they did. Sergeant-Tracker Alexander Riley was first Aborigine to receive a King's Police and Fire Service Medal for distinguished service in Canberra: Reginald William Saunders becomes the first Aboriginal lieutenant in the Australian Army in November 1944.

Alec Ross spent part of his life at Alice Springs Telegraph Station. His great grandfather was explorer John Ross, a Scottish bushman who chose the site of the Telegraph Station in 1871. Alec was born at Mosquito Creek in 1936. At the age of three, he was taken from his mother and taken to 'The Bungalow' at Alice Springs, a home for 'mixed race' children. First set up in 1914 for a part-aboriginal woman Topsy Smith, who drove a horse and buggy into Alice Springs with eleven of her children and a herd of goats, after her husband's death at the Arltunga mining fields, The Bungalow was moved to the Old Telegraph Station in 1932.

Alec Ross remembers the height of the military build-up in early 1942, when more than fifty trains a week were arriving in Alice Springs. Aboriginal people were employed to help foster the war effort by loading and unloading trains, sinking wells, building fences etc. and the Telegraph Station was needed to house these workers. So the children were moved out and transported north to a Methodist Mission on Croker Island, off the coast of Arnhem Land, 200 miles north-east of Darwin. 'Once we got on the island, it was just go mad. I thought it was paradise, truly. When I grew up, I think it was the best place I had ever been. We grew all our own food and grew everything we wanted. And we had horses, wild horses and ponies and pigs and goats, all running wild.'

After school each day, the boys learned farming, while the girls did baking and housework, as well as milking the goats. Three weeks after they arrived, the Japanese bombed Darwin. 'They flew over us every morning. The Japanese raids intensified and a message came that a boat was being sent to evacuate the Europeans but the children would stay until after the wet season. Three young women missionaries, Margaret Somerville, Jess March and Olive Peake chose to stay behind with their 'half-castes'. Suddenly accommodation was found near Sydney for the children. The Methodist Mission boat *Larrpan* arrived to take 95 children, missionaries, some lay people and a newborn baby to the mainland.'

Alec describes how the mission boat went to Barclay Bay and they walked to Pine Creek, mosquito infested country, drinking water from muddy holes and buffalo wallows, cooking on kerosene cans over an open fire, eating mostly rice and jam. They had to cross the South Alligator River, putting the Chevrolet Ute, with supplies, on a small punt and the kids clambered on, with some older ones swimming alongside. Margaret Somerville, who helped take care of the kids, was only twenty years old. She wrote about the trip in her book *They Crossed a Continent*. The American soldiers stationed at Pine Creek did not know she was a missionary, she was so sunburnt. 'Gee, she's well educated.' they said. At three in the morning, they were put on uncleaned cattle trucks to Larrimah and then to Alice Springs by road. At Birdum they were put on Australian Servicemen convoys and each soldier took one or more kids under his wing. At Alice Springs, they stayed at the Old Telegraph Station for a few days. A number of Aborigines suddenly appeared in the hills surrounding the Bungalow, all painted up, and just standing around. The children went on The Ghan to Adelaide then up to Sydney. Alec and the younger ones went to Otford, the older ones to Wollongong. They stayed from 1942 to 1946, when 69 of the original 95 returned with

A Carefree War

Margaret Somerville, on the *Reynella*. They were all so excited to get back to Croker Island, because that was their home. Alec stayed for another five years before he was told to go out to work. 'For the remaining five years I was at Croker, we did fencing, building houses. We had three or four hundred head of cattle to feed us. I mean, you couldn't wish for a better man than Rupert Kentish. He was a lay missionary. Hard worker. He taught me how to work and I can tell you, he worked the guts out of us really. On the island, when I left school, Mr Kentish or someone said, 'you've got to go to work.' So they took me to work. And from then on, I never looked back, really, because he taught us how to work hard. I remember getting flogged once for forgetting to feed the chooks. But then, I only thought later, he did it for my own good. He said, 'How would you like it if you had no water?' And that's true.

An article in the *Australian Women's Weekly* dated 29 December, 1945, says in part, in a slightly surprised tone: 'Seventy half-caste aboriginal children, innocent victims of fate and war, are soon to start an adventure designed to bring them pride and happiness. They will be the first occupants of a colony for half-caste waifs established by the Methodist Mission on Croker Island, north of Darwin. The missioners plan to educate and instruct as many half-caste children as possible until they can fill an accepted place in Australia's community life. They are now living at Otford. They were moved in June 1942. They have learned to read, write, sing and paint alongside the white children of Otford's residents. For three years the white children accepted their new classmates without question. Six of the half-caste girls have attended Wollongong High School, and eight older girls went into domestic service. Many of the children were despised and unwanted waifs. One, Marjorie, a nine year old of Javanese aboriginal blood, was rescued from a sordid opium den in Darwin. Because she was threatened with violence if she spoke or cried, she made herself dumb. When the children first came to Otford, many knew no other names than those the missioners had bestowed on them. Some of the girls changed their Mission Christian names to those of their favourite film stars. One child, baring a striking resemblance to Claudette Colbert, insists on being called 'Claudette'. Until they began to mingle with the white children, the half-castes did not know the meaning of birthdays. So 70 random dates were chosen for them. Mr Greentree, who taught the half-castes for two and a half years, considers their intelligence is as high as that of any white children. All of them show very high musical and artistic ability. Wollongong Domestic Science School wished to put these girls into a special class, but the Mission authorities suggested they attend classes with white pupils. The half-caste girls had topped their classes in art, physiology and English'

A Miss Mary Smith, a teacher at Otford, discovered Betty Fisher had a beautiful singing voice and gave her private lessons. Betty won a singing contest on the radio programme *Australia's Amateur Hour* for singing *Curly Headed Baby*. In 1946 Minister for the Interior, Mr Johnson said Betty was too young for a singing career (she was 14) and although she had been offered £25 a week for singing engagements, she should return to Croker Island and finish her schooling. She went back to Darwin and then to Croker Island on HMAS *Kangaroo*.

By June 1948, Australians read how Betty Fisher, whom the Press described as a 'half caste aboriginal singer', would bring her two month old baby, Shirley with her from Croker Island Mission to stay with a businessman and his wife in Adelaide. They would take her to Melbourne to further her career, to live with the businessman's sister. The businessman, as her manager, said she was so shy; she would need lessons in deportment. She received fan letters from all over Australia welcoming her chance to sing. Everything was set in place, but Betty suddenly left the home of the business couple and went to a half caste's compound to wait for Bob Shepherd, the father of Shirley.

She married in August 1948 still torn between a desire for a career and her daughter and marriage. 'My daughter means more to me than any microphone,' she said. 'There are no firm plans for the future.' Betty disappeared from the pages of the newspapers. She did not continue on in the limelight, but in those times of discrimination, it was remarkable that she got so far.

Joyce Dukes, softly spoken, and calm sits chatting with her lifelong friend Cassie Thornley, who lived next door when they were children. Joyce proudly showing photos of her grown up children, all working in interesting areas.

A Carefree War

My father Edward was born at Borroloola, Northern Territory. His mother was a traditional woman and his father a Chinese cook, Charlie Ah'Wong. At an early age he was taken to Roper River Mission, Eastern Arnhem Land and named Herbert. He was also adopted into the Mara tribe. Roper River, now *Ngukurr*, was established about 1908 as a safe haven for mixed race children, the traditional land owners, who were in danger of being killed by cattle graziers in the Gulf country. My mother Priscilla was born to a tribal woman and her father was a white stockman, Scottish, at the Alexandra cattle station in Queensland in 1908. Her tribal country is Eliott NT and her tribe is Jingilic.

I was born in 1934 at the Roper Mission and I had a brother, Alfie. We were not allowed to speak any of our traditional languages. The missionaries discouraged interaction with relatives outside the Missions and they used to regularly move some of their flock up to Groote Eylandt, on the Emerald River. They found on one of these moves that my mother was suffering from Hanson's disease, (leprosy). My brother Alfie and I were at Roper River with our father. At that time, I was eight. My mother was cured in a clinic in Darwin and remained there, becoming a nurse. She was there when the Japanese bombed it. After Darwin was bombed, it was feared the Japanese would invade using Roper River to isolate the top half of Australia by cutting off the Stuart Highway. Thousands of servicemen were stationed in the area.

I was caught up in this panic and sent away. The last time I saw my father was when he lowered me and my brother into a boat. But first Alfie and I went to see my mother. Actually I could hardly see as I picked up sandy blight on the bumpy ride there in the back of an army truck, and my mother greeted me with a blindfold around my eyes.

The Alice was so overcrowded that we were loaded onto the Ghan, which only had a few passenger cars. As it was not considered desirable for Aboriginal people to travel in those, we were put into empty cattle trucks, not cleaned out and I remember the smell all the way to Adelaide. I eventually found myself at an historic rectory of St Thomas' Church, which became the Church Missionary Society's Half-Caste Home at Mulgoa, ten miles from Penrith, NSW. My mother found a job at Winbourne Guest House nearby.

The social experiment of allowing 'half caste' children to mix with 'white people' worked very well. For seven years, the rectory had echoed to the laughter and footsteps of the children, then the news came from the Department of the Interior that the girls were to be sent to St Mary's Hostel, Alice Springs and the boys to the St Francis Hostel for Inland Boys at Semaphore, South Australia.

We didn't want to go, we were happy at the Mission, welcomed by the local community and I loved Penrith High School. I was the class captain and I wanted to be a doctor.

Joyce's mother, Mrs Tess Herbert was reported in The *Australian Women's Weekly* of 12 February, 1949, as saying that she had been taken to the Roper Mission as a young child, to work in the vegetable garden and fell timber, but would have liked to be a nurse. Although the children were taken south as a temporary wartime measure, they valued the chances to achieve they would never have had at Alice Springs. There were twenty silver cups on the sideboard, won by the children in athletics and they were planning careers. Tears fell at the thought of leaving their hopes and friends behind. Although a 'free citizen', able to vote, and a valued worker, Joyce's mother was not allowed to raise her own daughter, because Joyce was a ward of the state. There was a lot of protest. Penrith Chamber of Commerce campaigned for their stay. The Teacher's Federation protested for the first time as an organisation against segregated schooling. The Aboriginal Progress Association appointed Bill Ferguson to liaise with the Church authorities, but they were adamant. The state government sided with the church. Politicians like ex-Labour PM Billy Hughes 'Doc' Evatt, and the noted aboriginal tenor Harold Blair, all joined in the heated discussions. Mr P H Moy, Director of Native Affairs said, 'they were being sent away because they don't belong down here.' Joyce:

I can't say anything bad about the Mission, which was set up to protect children and women in need', but when the bus came to take us away, Mr Roberts, a supervisor, pulled me aside and said,' don't ask questions, Joyce, but run as fast as you can to your mother.' I ran for my life, whilst twenty- one crying and screaming children were loaded onto the bus. My escape from the authorities was front page news and in the media for some time.

Mr Johnson, the Minister for the Interior, bowed under pressure from the Australian people and Joyce was allowed to stay with her mother in January 1949. She had been staying with a friendly family at Pymble, because the police were looking for her. In the social upheaval of wartime, the United Nations had published the *Declaration of Human Rights* and migrants and refugees were arriving in boats, the assimilation question arose and Joyce's fight to be with her mother was a key part of it.

WWII was on such a massive scale, (an estimated 50 to 80 million deaths) that refugees flooded in from everywhere and were given special treatment. The difference in attitude between refugee and 'half-caste' children in their own country was pointed out. The phrase in the Press that Aboriginal children were gaining 'an accepted place in Australia's community life' is an improvement in attitudes towards Aboriginal people, which would not have happened without evacuation.

Aboriginal women also gained new chances to explore what they could do.

Kath Walker (Oodgeroo of the tribe Noonuccal, Custodian of the land Minjerribah):

I joined the Australian Women's Army Service principally because I did not accept fascism as a way of life. It was also a good way for an Aboriginal to further their education. In fact there were only two places where an Aboriginal could get an education, in jail or the Army, and I didn't fancy jail. Everyone was very nice to me when I joined up. I became a switchboard operator.

The war changed the lives of all women.

Chapter 17

Cassie Thornley:

In our case there were the two obvious reasons why we were sent away: my Mother wishing to return to nursing, and Dad was very busy. Not only did he have to reorganise the factory for the 'war effort' with decreased staff, but he was also very active in the industrial organisation to which he belonged (Metal Trades Employers Association). These employers employed over one third of the state's working men. Which brings us to the matter of who knew what? Dad would certainly have been aware of what was really happening as he had lobbied Federal Ministers and had friends in 'high places'! But the government officials had to consult with these men in order to organise the system towards producing the necessary military hardware and there were many late night meetings. A third reason which caused him a problem was that we had always had a live-in maid, as did many families then. But by 1940 the Land Army women were being sent to the country, and women were being called into the factories to learn the machines. (I have an elderly cousin who worked in a factory; she loved it - much more fun than an office). It was very difficult to get house help (in fact we never had another maid, the war changed attitudes about that).

Chapter 18
Gday! Being a Host

How we all fitted into the house is a mystery to me now!

– Fay Knight

Chapter 18

What was it like being a host? Some people just said, 'What was it like? They were just there'. You couldn't ignore the frightened voice at the end of the phone - 'Is that you mum? Is that your Uncle Jim?' Many country people lived a very simple, hardworking life in the 1940s. There was usually plenty of good fresh tucker and they made their own amusements. Many evacuees told me they stayed a long time in the country, which indicates that everyone settled down happily together. The farmer's wife probably welcomed the company of a female relative. The children probably enjoyed showing the 'city kids' around the farm, letting them feed the chooks and ride horses, pick fruit and play hide and seek in the sunshine. How much better than lying fearfully in their beds watching searchlights chase each other over the skies.

Nev Polkinghorne:
> My family owned a fruit farm in Griffith, NSW, during the war. My two young cousins and their mother left Sydney at the height of the conflict and stayed with us until it was deemed safe to return to Sydney.

Albert Browne:
> Shirley was the second of the six children and their mother who came to Cowra to live with our family of four children and our parents, in a small two bedroom weatherboard house, and to go to the local school.
>
> Most of us children slept on the front veranda, which was only partly protected by canvas blinds. Some of us had opened out wheat bags as additional blankets during the winter. We had a wood fuel stove, an open fireplace, and a chip heater in the bathroom, a cold water supply and an outdoor sewered toilet in the backyard. I cannot remember how long they stayed with us.

Ann Knight:
> My mother's parents at Griffith took in a brother and sister from Sydney. The children were accompanied by their nanny, who was my mother's maternal aunt.

A Carefree War

Fay Knight takes up the story:

Our Auntie Wanda (Wanda Thorne) – my mother's sister –
never married but worked as a nanny and housekeeping jobs
when we knew her. At the time of the war, June 1942 – she was
nanny to two children – Veronica and John. And if my memory
is still correct, they lived in an apartment in Macquarie Street
(The Astor) in Sydney and had wealthy parents. To us four farm
kids, their clothes were so good and lovely, and they were so
different to us, yet wonderfully warm and friendly and I'm sure
they enjoyed their six weeks stay (as I remember). The war to
us was something happening a long way off – and it made the
demand for fruit and vegies good and our farm prospered and we
all worked hard. Dad employed an Italian worker, Angelo, and
allowed him to build a home down past the Lucerne paddock
near a water drain channel. He had a wife and some small
children. The prices for fruit and vegies were good because of
the war and I guess it helped pay off our mortgage to the Water
Council and Irrigation Commission.

I was 14 years old when the submarines came in. Auntie Wanda,
Veronica and John would have come up from Sydney to Griffith
in the old steam train – overnight probably - and Dad would have
gone in our car to collect them as we were only a mile away, in
Griffith. Our farm was 40 acres, first farm near big main canal
(for irrigation) on the Yenda Road. Our gate was on a side road,
Farm 638, and over the built up part of railway line. When you
came in our farm gate, there was our driveway to our home –
almond trees on one side, and orange trees on left side. Our house
was weatherboard and tin roof, surrounded by wire fence and two
gates, to enclose Mum's garden and lawn. We had plenty of water
for irrigation as a ditch with a Detheridge Waterwheel up near
the gate for the water wheel reading man to see easily and send an
account for how much water the farm had used.

Our home only had two bedrooms, a good size lounge room,
bathroom and pantry and Dad had built on at side, a good kitchen

and back veranda to the laundry down the steps. How we all fitted in to the house is a mystery to me now! Mum and Dad had the main bedroom, while the four girls (Gwen, Ruth, Brenda and Peg) shared the other bedroom and as we got older, Gwen slept on front veranda, enclosed with canvas blinds and I slept on the side veranda, which was about twelve feet by twelve feet, so beds could go in there. This veranda had mosquito wire for side walls. Maybe Auntie Wanda and two city kids shared the bedroom.

We all rode bikes to school – and it'd be sure that Veronica and John went with us to school. Veronica probably in my class (I was in second year at Griffith High School) and Johnny at Yoogali Primary school – a mile down Yenda Road – now called McKay Road and three classrooms, three teachers (Mrs Lane – WWI widow and farm, first and second class), Mr Jones (left for air force) third and fourth class and Mr Bowditch (fifth and sixth class, lived in the school house) with family and his wife taught us sewing. I can't say I remember anyone else having 'city kids' to stay at this time. Veronica and John probably only came because our Auntie Wanda could bring them to us from the crisis in Sydney in 1942.

We all had a great time together – Mum and Auntie Wanda would have been busy with cooking and the house jobs etc. I'm sure we went out a lot - my father loved going out and visiting when time allowed. We had three lots of uncles and aunties in Griffith – all returned soldiers from WWI - on farms and our cousins to play with, too. The town of Griffith, in the Murrumbidgee Irrigation Area, was built for returned soldiers and a wonderful place to grow up in. As all men on the farms had been to war, they were great mates and helped each other in times of need and sickness. During WWII my Dad helped form a VDC group (1940) – 'old soldiers' – not supposed to be over 40 or so – formed in country towns and prepared to defend Australia – always going off for weekend training to Sydney, Katoomba, Wagga and Yenda and they marched in the Anzac Day parade up Banna Avenue to the memorial. I was so proud of him.

Never had relations and friends been so important nor had such an important task as caring for the small children been given such precedence. School students in small communities in country towns were told to be on their best behaviour because they were representing their school. They were expected to talk quietly when outside, walk in a crocodile going from one place to another, mind their manners and contribute to the local community by joining choirs, giving concerts and taking part in athletics or cricket. Friendships were formed that lasted for a lifetime, and some people moved back to the site of their evacuation to settle down and have their families. Two interviewees in this book returned to Armidale from Sydney because they did not enjoy the heat and revelled in Armidale's crisp, dry climate.

Gillian Branagan with her brother and mother in a gig

Bruce Whitfield enjoying the country

*Queenie Ashton, (Blue Hills), with
two of her children in Armidale*

Dear mum

We had a black out last night.
My choclats did not melt in the train
and I have only had to to or three so far
My heels are better,
I have bought a lote of books
We went down to a cricet pitch yesterday
and had a game
I would much rather be at Amoroo than at
school.
We have great fun ~~waste~~ watching trains
It is raining to day and we can't go out
side I do not want my paints.
The food is ok.
Love from
Geoff

Love Geoff - Children wrote letters home to their parents

Rob Whalley and his three sisters at Jessie Street, Armidales

Lynton Bradford with Gwen on his last trip to Boat Harbour

Vola Robertson (later Howe) was evacuated to Victoria from the Dandenongs

John Martin catching a lift

Peter Coles Andrews at the Fragars

John Martin at Casterton

John Martin - the happiest time of his life

Peter and Warren Daley were sent to stay with their
Aunt Eileen for nearly three years, 1941

*Warren and Peter Daley. Aunt Eileen referred to them as
'my boys' for the rest of her life, 1943*

Fay Sulman aged two years at Burragorang Valley NSW 1942

Fay Sulman with her host family at Burragorang

Kerry Packer as an evacuee

Alec Ross in 2003

*Betty Fisher with little Shirley
and her friend Annie*

Sir John Carrick, Minister of Education helped Joyce and stayed lifelong friends

The Church Missionary Society's Half-caste Home at Mulgoa,
ten miles from Penrith, NSW

Joyce Herbert with mother, Tess

The Press photo of pretty Joyce as a teenager riding a white pony captured hearts

Alan Wilkinson happily collecting rubber tyres for the war effort

THIS PROBLEM OF SENDING YOUR CHILD AWAY

Doctors discuss raid effects on youngsters of all ages

By MARGARET RICHARDS

"I don't know which would make me more unhappy —bombs or leaving mummy and daddy and living with people who don't really love me."

This is what a little girl of ten years told me when I asked her if she was going to be evacuated to the country.

THE psychological turmoil of this small child is only one of the problems of evacuation. Parents are trying to make up their minds just what to do.

Difficult pros and cons of the domestic side have to be weighed.

There is the desire of the wife to share with her husband whatever danger may come, the financial burden of supporting two households, and the uprooting of children from schools where they have already found their feet.

But, actually, these problems are only minor in relation to determining the mental and physical well-being of the children.

Some interesting opinions on the evacuation of children have been expressed by doctors.

A well-known Sydney medical man, in planning the evacuation of children, stated that all children under 12 should be evacuated, and at once. At the Government's expense, if necessary.

He considers that the average child, older than 12, has passed the fatally impressionable age.

An English doctor, Dr. W. E. R. Mons, a trained psychologist, is heartily in favor of the evacuation of children, no matter what their age.

He vigorously attacks the conduct of thousands of parents who have taken their children back from safe evacuation districts to their own homes in target areas.

"If there's another raid, the children can be evacuated again," is the dangerous outlook of the parents which he condemns.

But the effect of that one "extra" raid may do untold harm to the child.

It is impossible to tell immediately what reaction will result. Very possibly, the child himself will not know.

In one case cited by Dr. Mons, a boy had, according to his own statement, slept through a raid, but the realisation next day of how near death he had been caused a severe shock, none the less serious because it was delayed.

Like adults, children "crack hardly," and their casual air of assumed normality may be far removed from the real psychological reaction.

Besides, that one "extra" raid may undo in a few moments all the curative value of months in districts out of the line of fire.

Difficult children

WE heard much at the beginning of the war regarding "difficult evacuation children" in England, and no doubt many of us have wondered if families offering accommodation in Australia to city children would be faced with the same problems.

But these difficulties were not necessarily the children's fault. Some of them, of course, would be "difficult" even in their normal life and normal environment. In their own homes they would be looked on, as "unmanageables."

But the majority of the "difficult evacuation children" were "difficult" only because of their subjection to bombing—or, almost equally important—because of their subjection to the fear of bombing.

It was found that formerly good and intelligent children became suddenly obstreperous, destructive, mischievous, lazy, played truant from school, and, in short, unmanageable in the billet to which they had been evacuated.

In some cases, the teacher of the new school expressed doubt about the pupil's mental normality, where the previous report had stated him to be up to "scholarship standard."

The children also showed marked inability to know what to do with themselves.

They tired of one thing after another in rapid succession—legitimate amusement and mischief both proving equally lacking in attraction after a few minutes.

The children became a nuisance to themselves as well as to others.

They seemed to possess deep resentment against the adults who had failed to provide that security and protection which is every child's birthright; the collapse of all the values which education had carefully built up so far.

Death became a personal problem, and parental authority was no longer a safe shield against the direct threat of extinction.

Such problems are affecting British children who were previously normal—healthy, intelligent, well-behaved—and they are problems which will affect Australian children unless they are removed in time from our danger zones.

The strain of parting with parents to take up a new life with possibly critical strangers is difficult for children.

Those who have offered their homes and those who will be helping with evacuated children will have to remember that, whether subjected to air raids or not, the children will need infinite sympathy and understanding.

EVACUATION rehearsals are in full swing at Sydney day nurseries. Miss C. Hamilton, one of the voluntary workers at the Woolloomooloo nursery, with three of the 600 children who will be evacuated in the event of emergency.

ENGLISH MOTHERS sadly say farewell to their children en route to areas safe from bombing.

Do you know your Hollywood?

Informative session from 2GB

Many Australian stage and radio stars will appear in the new 2GB programme, "Radio Hollywood," which recently had its first presentation from the Macquarie Auditorium.

Among the artists who will make their bow are Janet Lind, former star of Louis Levy's Gaumont-British symphony orchestra; Alan Coad, regarded as one of the finest baritones in Australia; Joan Hatton, the Australian Deanna Durbin; Ron Randell, Billy Samuel, the American comedian; and George Blackshaw.

ONLY a year ago, George Blackshaw was a serious and austere radio announcer in Melbourne. Now he is regarded highly as a comedian, one of his most popular acts being his discussions on music which he calls "Highbrow talks for lowbrows."

The Hollywood Reporter, who is one of Australia's leading movie authorities, provides three items in the programme. The first is news and gossip from Hollywood, received each week by cable. The second is a "Movie Quiz,"

in which contestants ask him a question dealing with the movies. If he fails to answer correctly the contestant receives five shillings.

The contestant is then asked a question and, if successful, receives another five shillings. A bonus of an extra ten shillings goes to the contestant who scores in both.

His third feature is "Country and Interstate Quiz," in which listeners outside Sydney send in questions they would like the Hollywood Reporter to answer. For each question used 2/6 is paid, and if he cannot answer them spontaneously the writer receives 5/-.

Reg Lewis and his Macquarie Orchestra are responsible for the

THE Hollywood Reporter in front of the microphone.

musical side of the show, while Barbara James is the vocalist.

"Radio Hollywood" is produced by George Matthews, who studied production in Hollywood. It is heard from 2GB every Thursday at 7.45 p.m. Listeners are invited to witness these shows by applying to 2GB for free reservations.

Ian Murray Wilson (second row, second on right) at his one teacher school at Dalby

Ian Murray Wilson's brass identity tag for evacuation to Dalby

Bill Deeley attracting more mosquitoes than his brother Ron, 1942

MUNICIPALITY OF ERSKINEVILLE — EVACUATION REGISTER

The Council asks you to kindly fill in this Card and hand it to your Warden when he calls.
The information is required for N.E.S. and Evacuation purposes in case of severe bombing raids. Should any of the particulars whi
you have entered on this card alter at any time, kindly notify the Town Clerk, Erskineville. You are asked to treat this matter
URGENT in the interests of your own and your neighbours' safety.

Name of Street... *Sydney Street* .... House No... *4* .... 'Phone No. (if any)........

Occupier's Surname... *Evline Pearl* .... Christian Names... *Evline Pearl Macfad*
(IN BLOCK LETTERS)

PARTICULARS OF PERSONS RESIDING ON PREMISES.
(Names to be arranged in order of age—eldest first).

Surname (BLOCK LETTERS)	Christian Names	Sex	Age in Years	Religion (optional)	Occupation	State o Health
MacFADYEN	*Evline Pearl*	*Female*	50	*C. England*	*Office Work*	*not co g*
MacFADYEN	*Horace* ✗	*male*	33	*C. Efland*		
MacFADYEN	*Ronald.*	*male*	29	*C. England*	*Labour*	
MacFADYEN	*Norman* ✗	*male*	25	*C. England*		
MacFAYEN	*Doris*	*femal*	27	*C. England*	*Housework*	*not - g*
JEFFERIES	*Catherine*	*femal*	70	*Catholic*	*Housework*	*no go*

PARTICULARS OF PREMISES.

Number of floors... *2* .... No. of Bedrooms... *4* .... No. of Living Rooms... *1*

No. of Verandahs for Sleeping-out Purposes... *none* .... No. of Beds, Stretchers, etc. *four beds take*

Particulars of Garages, Sheds, etc.....................

This Section to be filled in by Occupiers of Premises other than Dwelling Houses.

Name of Street... *Sydney Street* .... Number... *4* .... 'Phone No. (if any).......

Nature of Business... *Office Cleaning* .... No. of Rooms... *4* .... No. of Floors... *2*

Evacuation Register card, Erskineville

*The boarders of St Vincent's at Potts Point settled
in at Wahgunyah guesthouse, Katoomba*

Chapter 19
Victorian Evacuees

I remember great excitement at school because one little girl was evacuated from Alice Springs, which we felt was very close to the war. We sewed handkerchiefs for soldiers and we thought she should be given one!

– Shirley Davies

A Carefree War

The *Standard* (Frankston), January 1942, complains: 'Many people are suffering from an evacuation complex - a word which has become too common in our plan of life. It's spoken as a matter of course, as though it is the only thing to do - evacuate. If needs be, children must be evacuated; that is obvious; also the aged and infirm, but why anyone else?'

Mrs Vola Howe (nee Robertson):

I am now 85 years and with my mother and three siblings evacuated from Scott Street, Dandenong to live for about 18 months in Maldon Victoria. My parents were frightened that the Japs were coming South! My Mum was especially scared as where we lived in Dandenong in Scott Street there was a petrol dump down the road and Mum was quite sure they would come and bomb it! My father boarded in Brunswick where he worked making trailers for the war effort. I was 12 years old when we moved and transferred from Dandenong High School to Castlemaine High - they didn't have higher than Primary in Maldon. I was the eldest with two brothers and a baby sister, in 1941 when the fear was that Japan had attacked Darwin and concern they were coming south! We eventually moved back, and my father was sick of travelling each weekend by train to see us. My mother kept the car with us in Maldon to get around in!

Shirley Davies was at Frankston Primary School during the war:

I remember great excitement at school because one little girl was being evacuated from Alice Springs, which we felt was very close to the war. We all wanted to be her friend and give her things. We sewed handkerchiefs for soldiers and we thought she should be given one!

Myrna McBain lived in Richmond:

I was born in October 1940 at East Melbourne the first child of Elsie (Williams) and Frank Jones and they lived in Richmond. At this time my father worked for a tannery in Richmond and was exempt from war service. My mother had grown up in Lilydale.

Chapter 19

Richmond, Victoria was a factory area and Lilydale was rural. I am guessing some time in 1942, my mother and I went to stay with her parents in Lilydale. A brother of my father had enlisted in the RAAF in January 1942 from Sydney where he lived at Quakers Hill. He was married and had a son born in January 1941. He left Sydney for Melbourne and was at Ascot Vale before leaving Melbourne in May 1942 for 'the islands'. This was probably when his wife and son came down from Sydney, and stayed with my father in Richmond to look after him. My recollection is that my cousin slept in my cot and my Aunt used a lot of my mother's preserves, jams etc. and they left Sydney for Melbourne as it was felt to be safer. Also Lilydale was safer than the factories of Richmond if the Japanese bombed it.

My mother and I were definitely back in Richmond when my sister was born in April 1944 and my Aunt back in Sydney when her second son was born in May 1945. My uncle returned to Australia in December 1943.

Mrs Bassett-Smith:

> I was an evacuee and I went not because of invasion fears but because my father was away with the AIF. I had a governess with a friend's family at Eltham. In the thirties, it was not unusual for a governess to be part of a country family and stay on for years. I don't remember being frightened and I don't think Victorians feared an invasion because of the topography of their coastline. I thought air raid drill was fun. One of the evacuees with us had her home in Sydney shelled by the Japanese.

Elizabeth Paine from Brighton Historical Society along the same lines:

> We do not have a lot of information. One of our volunteers was a student teacher in 1942, the Hyde Street, Footscray School suburb of Melbourne. Her job was preparing the identification tags for the children to prepare for evacuation. Some children had to be sent to a cleansing station. Fortunately the evacuation did not have to take place. Some schools were relocated at short notice at the beginning of the war for servicemen's use of their buildings.

Melbourne Girl's Grammar School at South Yarra was evacuated for Air Force use. Some girls went to Marysville, some to Doncaster, some had governesses. East Melbourne St Catherine's was evacuated to Warburton, the vacated building used as a WAAAF training base.

A Dr Weigall from the Bush Nursing Association said in January 1942 that evacuee children were in greater danger in small country towns because if the enemy dropped incendiary bombs in dry forest or pastoral areas, fire could be life threatening.

In 1946 although much material was censored and not available, armchair strategists reviewed the evidence and offered opinions. In August 1946, the *Brisbane Worker* reported the Minister for Information, Mr Calwell, saying at an election meeting in the Melbourne Town Hall: 'The threat of a Japanese invasion at Port Phillip Bay through Bass Strait was very real on Boxing Day, 1941. So near was the danger he said, 'that the officer in charge of defence for Victoria sent urgent messages to municipal councils calling in old German howitzers, given as souvenirs after the First World War' Mr. Calwell strongly attacked the Menzies and Madden Governments for Australia's unpreparedness for war with Japan. The howitzers were rushed to Maribyrnong to be rebored and used for defence and one division was stationed each side of the Bay. 'Australia was 300,000 rifles short at the time,' he said.

Chapter 20
Aftermath

My father put his arms under my mother's coat and hugged her and I started crying and bit him on the leg. 'Leave my mother alone.' I sobbed. I'm sure this happened to many children.

– Ann Howard

Peace. Everyone wanted to make a noise! Boys on bikes dragged tins around, in country towns a piano was hoisted onto a horse and cart, people hanging onto the sides singing and whooping. Someone belted a rainwater tank with a stick.

Private Siggins was the first mother to join the services. She said:
'I have two sons in the AIF and a son-in-law POW. My husband is with the Allied Works Council in Darwin. I just feel I am doing my duty. We must all help in this war for freedom and honour, justice and truth. I feel that it is women like me who should do so just as much as younger women. I've brought up my family and so now I am free. This is just as much my job as my husband's. We both feel like that.'

When peace was declared, 66,000 women were demobbed. The first AWAS were posted solely to headquarters and base installations, later serving in intelligence, signals, ciphers, electrical and mechanical training units, heavy convoy work, anti-aircraft and coastal artillery, gunsights and searchlights, as cooks, clerks, orderlies, canteen workers, provosts, butchers, instrument repairers, transport drivers and ambulance drivers. Some were attached to chemical warfare experimental units, some administrators; some fixed marine engines, some interpreters, some entertainers. Some repaired bomb blasted tanks from the Middle East, some were First Aid experts. Women had new ideas, skills and aspirations. Women who had the responsibility of home duties, and women in the war effort were all changed. If they resumed the role of mother and wife without an outside career, they passed on their thoughts to their daughters and when their children were past primary school age, applied for study or jobs.

Did men's attitude change? Old habits die hard. A taxi driver on seeing a servicewomen's uniform remarked, 'Who's going to do your thinking for you now?'

Women found a lack of real choice in post war Australia. One ex-servicewoman I spoke to had missed a lot of schooling to help with her brother, who was an epileptic, while her parents ran a small shop in the Blue Mountains. An intelligence test the Army gave her revealed her intelligence. 'You should be at university,' she was told. 'What's that?' she replied. She did gain a place in university and became an academic, but it was hard for women to receive further training, war had proved a very expensive exercise for Australia. From 1946 to 1947, the amount of pensions paid out from two world wars was fifteen and a half million pounds, to incapacitated members of the forces and their dependants. In 1945, a Medical Benefits Scheme was introduced and benefit was paid for people with TB. Child endowment was raised to 75 shillings a week. Widows with one or more dependent children received seven pounds ten a week. Generous maternity allowances reflected the desire to populate or perish. WWI widows were not allowed to work to supplement their meagre pensions, but WWII widows were. Returning ex-servicemen had priority in regaining their old jobs or getting new ones.

Housing was at a premium and building materials scarce. The government had made no provisions for returning servicemen and women wanting to have a family. People lived in garages, tents, and paid key money for poor quality rented housing. It was almost impossible to save and to exist on a small farm was challenging.

Men returned sadder and wiser, sometimes traumatised. Towards the end of the war Australia's interests were not served as MacArthur committed Australians to 'mopping up' campaigns against the Japanese, of doubtful strategic value, and costly in Australian lives. More than 31,000 Australians were prisoners of war. The German camps were the responsibility of the Luftwaffe and usually the prisoner's biggest challenge was boredom, although the seriousness of this should not be underestimated. The Asian camps were places of inhuman working demands and unbelievably terrible living conditions, with starvation diets and brutal guards. A third of Australian prisoners failed to survive clearing the jungle and building the 320 kms of railway to link Burma and Thailand. The survivors suffered for the rest of their lives. Australian crowds meeting the rescued men at the wharves fell silent as they saw their emaciated bodies and many wept. Some of them had lied about their age to enlist and were only sixteen years old. There was a lingering distrust of the Japanese when the Australians saw how their men had suffered as they came home as returning prisoners of war. One woman described to me how she visited a friend for tea, who apologised for having a Japanese tea set.

'We bought it before the war.'

They had been right to fear a Japanese invasion. Women met men unrecognisable as their husbands and were not offered counselling, general practitioners being untrained. GP's advice was to put on a pretty dress, hum and smile a lot, resulting in domestic violence and divorce. The dog would glance at his master's face, the first one to know something was wrong, ready to run under the table. Men with really bad experiences were unable to talk about it except to their mates. They retreated into their own world. It was generally accepted that the war should not be mentioned. The children who had been more or less carefree through the war years, found the strange male intruder into their home disturbing, especially when he was violent towards their mother in his traumatised state, when they had lived quite happily with her all to themselves for several years. I was four years old when I met my father, coming home to London in strange smelling khaki, with boots. My Mother and I went to the station to meet him. It was in turmoil, with men pouring off the train, being greeted with screams, laughter and tears, some men walking past their loved ones like ghosts. My father put his arms under my mother's coat and hugged her and I started crying and bit him on the leg. 'Leave my mother alone.' I sobbed. I'm sure this happened to many children.

Wives of returning servicemen wanted a peaceful, happy home, but dealing with trauma is complicated and they were not equipped to do anything but try and avoid confrontation and bear the bad times stoically. There were no professional counsellors or marriage guidance officers until the 1950s. The level of divorce increased by 55% from 1944 to 1947. In 1947, there were 8,000 divorces. Of course this is against the unusually high rate of hasty war marriage, but significant because it was difficult for women to exist alone, especially with dependent children, so they did not leave lightly. It was not socially approved to get a divorce.

Chapter 20

Women had been brought up for marriage, not to leave marriage. The high rate of divorce reflects a high level of misery. Some returned servicemen had nightmares, could not bear being indoors, were frightened of open spaces, making it difficult to settle down to work. Children, who had a more or less 'carefree war', happy on farms with loving relatives, came home to a very different life in most cases. Couples who were able to greet each other lovingly and settle down were a rarity. The war left a legacy of problems. One evacuee who had no problems was little Judith Thurgood (Andrews), who was evacuated with brother, Peter to a farm near Bathurst when she was three years old:

> I caught the measles, or perhaps took them with me. My older cousin put me on a horse with the instruction: 'Hang on like grim death!' and we still laugh about that. My aunt took my brother gold panning and he still has a little bottle of gold bits from the Fish River. I never had any sense of being hungry, but after we returned home, life changed dramatically for everyone and there were shortages. Although being evacuated took mum away and we didn't see much of our father, I was made so much of by my aunt and uncle and cousins, that I only remember it as a wonderful experience.

Australia gained an independent political standing out of WWII. In hindsight, because Singapore was never supposed to fall, Australia had supported Britain in a military sense to its own disadvantage. In 1939 when Britain declared war against Germany, Prime Minister Menzies announced that we were therefore also automatically at war, without any consultative process. Menzies agreed to the Australian Navy being controlled by Britain as part of their Royal Navy, and committed Australia's Air Force to British command for use in Europe. Their main role was Australian crews to be used in the RAF, which later severely restricted our capacity to play an effective role in the Pacific War. In December 1941, when Japan attacked Pearl Harbour and then Singapore, Australia declared war on Japan without a British declaration.

The social fabric of Australia changed forever. Migrants were needed for building infrastructure like the Snowy Mountains Scheme. Australia started accepting refugees and displaced persons, post war social policy being dominated by migrants, the population almost doubling to 13 million from 1945 to 1975. Arthur Calwell coined the term 'New Australians' trying to supplant terms like 'bloody Pom', 'wop' and 'wog'.

It was the beginning of the end for 'White Australia' and the start of modern multiculturalism. Australia began communicating with the world and demanding good coffee and creative recipes. Australian war brides went to America and Australians embraced American films. Children sang songs with an American twang.

Another change was the concept of citizenship. During World War II everyone in Australia was issued with a personal identity card and required to report changes of address to the government, to help monitor Aliens (non-citizen residents), particularly non-Europeans and Asian residents. Prior to 1949, Australian citizenship did not exist as we know it today.

Buildings in Australia changed. Small country towns like Cairns had high rise buildings and an international airport. In 1946 James Hardie exhibited models of prize-winning asbestos-cement houses.

Children had learnt many things, some positive, some negative and were wise beyond their years. Some children, when they would have dared each other to jump a stream or gone scrumping, played with the deadly toys of war.

A great source of pride for Stan Gratte was finding himself in the *Geraldton Express,* 21 November, 1945 on the same page as famous war criminals. On the left of the page, the headline reads: Trials at Nuremberg, Nazi Leaders Arraigned, and The Opening Scenes. Two columns along, the headline says: Missing Explosives, Schoolboys in Court, Warning from the Bench.

Stan and some school mates found a sandbagged dugout with enough explosives to eliminate the radar station next to it. Radar was considered secret at that time as not every power possessed it. In case of an invasion, it was to be destroyed. The air force dumped bombs and ammunition past the Abrolhos Islands in deep water, several times a day, but the army forgot about the dugout.

One day, a boy brought a 1.5 kg slab of TNT to school and I bought it from him for two shillings. I was quite a capitalist as at that time I was working after school at Brandenburg's Pharmacy for ten shillings a week. The story about the dugout was no longer a rumour and a lot of boys soon knew about it. By the time I got there all the TNT and some gelignite had gone, but there were still plenty of pickings. Some boys must have been there a long time before, as much of the material was scattered about. For instance, I remember red electric detonators lying in the sand almost corroded away. To touch them almost certainly meant an explosion.

I took away fuses, detonators, gelignite and last but not least the plunger. I had some mates whose dad owned a goldmine near Wiluna and they were a great source of information on the technical details...they had introduced me to 'fracteur', which is the miner's name for gelignite, a long time previous. We had become expert demolishers of trees. I did a bit of swapping as I held all the key things, like detonators, which are necessary to explode the stuff, and of course the plunger and fuse. Didn't we have some fun! A few of us were riding our bikes along Brand Highway, heading for the Greenough River to do some fishing, using gelignite. I had seen about 50 boys scoot up the big sandhill nearby. I said to my mates, 'here watch this' Next thing, *Woomp*! The ground shuddered and a big black cloud of smoke and dust filled the valley. The boys had let off a slab of TNT in Berringer's old abandoned tannery pits. Those explosions always around the sandhills surrounding our present suburb of Mahomets, shook houses as far away as Gregory Street and no adult tipped what was happening because they had become accustomed to the Army using the area for trench mortar and machine gun practice.

Anyhow, all good things come to an end. A schoolboy hid a slab of TNT under an aquarium stand in his home. His Dad found it. The police rounded us all up. The RAAF was particularly keen to get the plunger. It had a serial number and needed to be accounted for. And I had that item. We appeared before the magistrate. Reformatory was an option. But almost all the explosives had been used and none went into the sea. There were more explosives than were owned up to. Our Headmaster, Mr Evans gave us a good reference and I'm sure that helped. He said we were 'exemplary pupils.' It was a great thing for a Headmaster to do for his pupils and indicative of that day and age. I well remember the Magistrate saying, after a long lecture, '...this is not the fault of these boys. Any red-blooded boy would have been into this. It is the fault of the men who left this stuff there.'

Last to appear before the magistrate was yours truly, about the plunger. They got that back, so I got off lightly with costs of only four shillings and sixpence. The boys who owned up to using the explosives paid costs of one pound and ten shillings each. We were not fined and we received no convictions, only a severe lecture. The last thing the magistrate said was, 'you all realise that you go from this court without a stain on your characters'. As the boys filed out of court, one of them said, 'Thank you Sir,' that was me. I was well brought up.

Vivid stories from these child evacuees come from looking back over seventy years, to when the war stopped being 'over there'. These voices from the past will soon be words from the past, but their firsthand accounts will keep their memories alive from between these pages. They were there when Australians watched the great carnage of WWII from a distance and then realised that the fingers of war were stretching out towards their homes. First there was the fear of bombing and shelling. Then it happened. Then there was the fear of parachutists and army boots striking the tarmac of their high streets. They had no idea where or when this would happen (neither did the Japanese!).

They fled from the coast, or steeled themselves to stay, sending their little ones away. Some people involved were famous names, like Queenie Ashton and Kerry Packer. Mostly they were mums and sometimes dads putting as much distance as possible between their children and the point of entry, wherever that was going to be, from the feared Imperial Japanese Army.

This history was slipping away and now they have had a chance to tell their stories within the pages of this book. Many Australians will be totally unaware that voluntary evacuation happened. The militarisation of war history is so pervasive, that a place has not been given to the frightened and threatened civilians of the time. People involved were so glad when the war was over, and had a new set of challenges with their returning traumatised menfolk, that everything was forgotten except building a new future. They had bravely hidden their feelings and smiled at their children.

David Tranter told me.

We were the lucky ones, kids born in 1929/30, too young to go to war but old enough to enjoy all the excitement.

They were the lucky ones, indeed, to enjoy A Carefree War.

CONTRIBUTORS

I interviewed many people for *A Carefree War* and have reproduced their accounts with their permission. I am conscious that these experiences were an important part of their lives, and I have endeavoured to give them a rewarding and accurate book. I would like to sincerely thank all of my contributors.

Altman, Jim

Atton, Cecily

Ayre, Patricia

Baker, Heather

Baskerville, Bruce

Bassett-Smith, Mrs

Bates, Miriam

Bates, Peter

Berry, Patricia

Bourke, Joan

Bradford, Lynton

Branagan, Gillian

Bretherton, James

Brown, Albert

Campbell, Elsie

Carolan, Ann

Carter, Lindsay

Coleman, Myfanwy

Coles, Peter (Andrews)

Crawford, Bruce

Craymer, Dick

Craymer, Joan

Creer, Jim

Curlewis, Ian

Cusins, George

Daley, Peter

David, Laeonie

Davis, Pam,

Deeley, Bill

Deveacke, Keith

Dobson, Martin

Dukes, Joyce

Ecob, Alan

Euwer, Anthony

Kyle, Andrew

Lark, Mary

Mackenzie, Sue

Macleay, Jean

Martin, Bill

Martin, John

McBain, Myrna

McCashney, Harold

McDonald, Valda

McFadden, Gordon

McKern, Don

Meaker, Arnold

Moss, Mary

Murphy, Kev

Newton, Georgia

Owen, Norman

Contributors

Paine, Elizabeth
Palmer, Sylvia
Parker, Jacqueline
Piaud, Charmaine
Polkinghorne, Nev
Potter, Geoff
Putt, Jane
Pye, Eileen
Featherstone-Haugh, Richard
Fisher, Cynthia
Fisher, Vera
Fletcher, Alan
Ford, Mary
Galwey, Alan
Gammidge, Colin
Geoghlin, Bill
Goldrick, Robert
Goldsmith, Horace
Goodhew, Ron
Gratte, Stan
Gray, Ann
Grieve, Judy
Grose, Peter
Gross, Audrey
Hanford, Meryl
Hanson, Jenny
Healy, Anthony
Hellmund, Marie
Hishion, Barry
Hoad, Geoff
Hooper, Tom
Howe, Vola
Huntsman, Leonie
Joiner, Margaret
Johnstone, Meryl

Killeen, Shirley
Kingston, Bev
Knight, Ann
Knight, Fay
Pringle, Michael
Reedman, Les
Riseley, Kate
Roper, Lance
Ross, Alec
Smith, Pamela
Squires, John
Stewart, Jenny
Sulman, Fay
Sun, Stella
Suttor, Judy
Taylor, Margaret
Taylor, Bob
Taylor, John
Thomas, Elaine
Thornley, Cassie
Tranter, David
Thurgood, Judith
Valder, John

About the Author

Ann Howard, originally from London, gives a voice to people to claim their own place in history - she has researched and written on drovers, child migrants, pioneer women, the AWAS in World War II and now has found a new hidden history - invasion fears and Australian child evacuees in the 1940s.

Through extensive research and interviewing, she has brought to life a subject never written about before - a time when people were so terrified of the Japanese taking over Australia, that they sent their children away from the coast and from key war areas, for a few months or sometimes three years.

Ann Howard loves life. She is an enthusiastic traveller and adventurer. She has ridden elephants through the Sumatran jungle; climbed Anak Krakatau when part of it was erupting; made 14,000 feet free-fall from a plane and rock climbed in Tahiti. She brings this enthusiasm to her writing and studying. Ann enjoys her grandchildren, her partner's musical gift, her dogs, garden and a good single malt; not necessarily in that order.

Ann lives in a heritage house she restored on Dangar Island in the Hawkesbury River, where the four-time, prize winning local histories she wrote are very popular. Ann's next book will be *You'll be Sorry!* about the AWAS in World War II.

Other books by Ann Howard:

The Bonsai Ballerina and other stories
A Ghost, a Murder & Other Dangar Tales
Ten Dry Pies & Other Dangar Tales
Rainbow on the River & Other Dangar Tales
Derrymacash to Dangar
Roads and Highways
Australia in WWI
Australia in WWII
Cattle Drovers
Coaches, Riverboats and Railways
Women in Australia
From Colonies to Commonwealth
A Century of 'Life' MML 1895-1995
You'll Be Sorry!
Where Do We Go From Here?
After Barnardo
C'mon Over!

Index

Index

Index

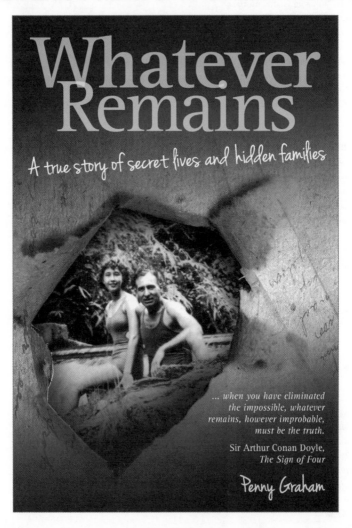

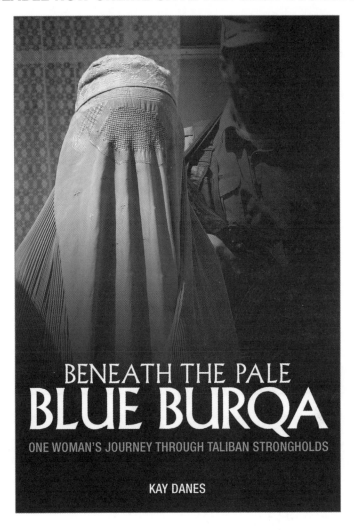

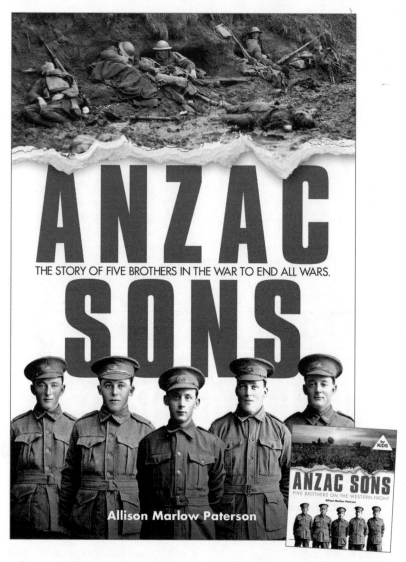